FATHERS IN PRISON

by Larry Wolfgang

DEDICATION

*This book belongs to my family
and students, friends who believed
in me before I believed in myself.
Thanks for the confirmation.*

*Love and peace,
Wolfman*

Library of Congress Catalog Number
99-93791

ISBN: 0-9671305-0-6

*Cover Artist: Robert Stickloon
Book Designer: Maureen A. Logan
Editor: Melissa Ingram*

Stone Creek Publishing
*RR2 Box 110 • Paxinos • PA 17860
Phone: 570.672.1111
Fax: 570.672.9411*

ON PARENTING

Your children are not your children.
They are the sons and daughters of Life's
    longing for itself.
They come through you but not from you,
And though they are with you, yet they belong
    not to you.
You may give them your love but not your
    thoughts,
For they have their own thoughts.
You may house their bodies but not their souls,
For their souls dwell in the house of tomorrow,
Which you cannot visit, not even in your
    dreams.
You may strive to be like them, but seek not
    to make them like you,
For life goes not backward nor tarries with
    yesterday.
You are the bows from which your children
    as living arrows are sent forth.
The archer sees the mark upon the path of
    the infinite, and He bends you
With his might that His arrow might go swift
    and far.
Let your bending in the archer's hand be for
    gladness,
For even as He loves the arrow that flies,
So He loves also the bow that is stable.

–Kahlil Gibran

ABOUT THE COVER

Larry and I became close friends and confidants during the year I worked as artist-in-residence at F.C.I. Schuylkill. Through this truly unordinary experience, we became kindred spirits in our attitudes toward the prisoners and our philosophies concerning their development—consciously avoiding bureaucratic rehabilitation. A number of inmates studied in both of our classes, and more than once, a discussion carried over from "Wolfman's" class, and a concept from parenting would manifest itself in their artwork. At first I was surprised, pleasantly I might add, at the absence of grossly overdeveloped super-heroines and other comic book and tattoo imagery. Instead, I heard feedback like, "I wish I could see my daughter's face when she sees this picture I painted for her"—a peaceful or fanciful landscape or a still life of her toys.

I am very proud to be asked by Larry to paint the cover art for this book because I'm thoroughly positive there is no one more qualified to have written it. Through his humble humanitarianism there will be a lot more thoughtful, loving, and effective fathers in the world, and consequently fewer incarcerated young men and women in future generations.

–Robert Stickloon
Artist

Preface

I write this book because I have heard the agony of over 800 incarcerated men, cries that I can no longer ignore. Most men never discuss fathering or relationship issues, especially with other men. This book is offered as a guide for men who want to learn more about fatherhood. I hope every man will quickly grasp the enduring impact he has on his children.

Students have told me that this material helped them to become better fathers from prison than they were on the outside. The commitment to our children is too important to neglect.

Hi! I am Larry Wolfgang. Pam and I have been married for nearly twenty-three years. We have two daughters; Angi is a college sophomore, and Andi is a junior in high school. My family is the most important gift of God. Every day I dream for my family and their future. I realize that my behavior adds something new to the story of my ancestors and descendants. I have graduate degrees in Marriage and Family, and Divinity.

Fathers, we are not perfect. We are ordinary men dedicated to our children and family because it is noble and right. The challenge is to be the best father we can be, overcoming barriers and obstacles.

Namaste is a Hindu expression that means, I honor you because you are a reflection of the divine. This is the highest symbol of respect we can offer each other. Place the palms together, thumbs against the chest, and nod slightly. Namaste!

ACKNOWLEDGEMENTS

Knowledge is a tree, born in the soil of human experience. Wisdom is her fruit. My incarcerated students have taught me about suffering and hope. Pam, who patiently read this book, teaches me about love. However, the crowning achievement of my life is being a father to Angi and Andi. Ancestors celebrate the birth of a new star. Angi and Andi are stars on the edge of the dress rehearsal called life. I have learned that I need them more than they need me.

Author's note: To protect the confidentiality of my students, I have changed the names and minor details of the stories. Also, I have interchanged the pronouns "he" and "she," and "him" and "her" to avoid a gender bias.

Table of Contents

ONE AND THE SAME

I'm frozen in time with nothing to do,
My emotions and feelings are surrounded by you.
The emptiness and heartbreak are feelings of pain,
This coldness reminds me of a driving, freezing rain.
The only way to rid this pain as such
Is the warmness of your breath, the softness of
    your touch.
Both of these thoughts seem so far away
That we'll have to wait 'til another day.
For now I rely on what's in your letters
Until the day that we're together.
I look at your pictures but can't touch or feel,
Although they are gorgeous, they are not real.
The glow of your face, the softness of your skin,
The goodness of your heart that comes from within,
These are the things that pictures don't show,
Everything that I miss, I hope that you know.
We are two and the same and need one another,
Like sisters and brothers, fathers and mothers.
I look to the future and see the riches of gold,
With you right by my side, as we grow old.
Always and forever is what I look for
Once I get out from behind these closed doors.
To hold you in my arms and whisper your name,
You and me are one and the same.

–Big Al

INTRODUCTION

Life is fragile. Our society depends on certain institutions like the home and school to teach children the value of relationships and life. As this happens, our community prospers because of mutual respect. On the other hand, if children do not learn respectful patterns of interaction at home, our community suffers.

Families, including absent fathers, shape the attitudes, values, perceptions, and habits of their children. Patterns learned at home are never forgotten but passed down to the next generation.

Five-year-old Matt runs up the steps and slams the bathroom door, cursing under his breath. He is too young to understand that his mother and stepfather's fighting will scar him for life. "Please, God, make it stop," Matt cries.

RESEARCH

Approximately one million, eight hundred thousand (1.8 million) persons are incarcerated in the United States (U.S. Dept. of Justice, 1999). Seventy percent (70%) of juveniles incarcerated in state reform institutions are from homes with no father or without natural parents (U.S. Dept. of Justice, Special Report, Sept. 1988). Eighty percent (80%) of rapists motivated by displaced anger come from fatherless homes (Criminal Justice & Behavior, Vol. 14, p. 403-26, 1978). Eighty-five percent (85%) of all children that exhibit behavioral disorders are from fatherless homes (Center for Disease Control). Seventy-five percent (75%) of homicide perpetrators come from single parent homes (Press Enterprise, Bloomsburg, Pennsylvania, Feb. 12, 1997).

According to a recent study by Cynthia Harper at the University of Pennsylvania and Sara S. McLanahan of Princeton University:

> Young men who grow up in homes without fathers are twice as likely to end up in jail as those who come from traditional two-parent families...those boys whose fathers were absent from the household had double the odds of being incarcerated--even when other factors such as race,

income, parent education and urban residence were held
constant (<u>Reuters News</u>, August 20, 1998).

Forty percent (40%) of all children do not live with their natural
father, and the number is growing. Research repeatedly indicates
that father neglect is the most significant factor toward delinquency
and crime (<u>Fatherless America</u>, David Blankenhorn 1995).

Father neglect injures the soul of our children. Frustrated
with the stresses of life and work, too many fathers ignore their
children instead of dealing with the limitations. These men do
not fully understand the effect of father neglect, perhaps because
of their own father's absence. Today, more than twelve million
fathers are not taking responsibility for their children (Mark Bryan,
"Oprah," Oct. 5, 1998).

This book is for incarcerated fathers. Children, with father-
hunger on their faces, occasionally spend two hours in the visiting room with a man they barely know. Teenage sons, bitter with
resentment and frustration, begin a life of dependency and delinquency because they have no idea how men fit into our society,
let alone family life. Teenage daughters, desperate for a father's
encouragement and affection, turn to their boyfriends for affirmation and end up pregnant, children having babies. Brokenhearted
wives struggle to make ends meet as they helplessly watch their
children self-destruct. And Dad, locked down in bitterness and
frustration, blames everyone, including himself, for failing.

The vast majority of incarcerated men never had a personal
relationship with their father, and now the cycle continues.
Eighty-five percent (85%) of all youth in prison grow up in
fatherless homes (Fulton County, Georgia; and Texas Dept. of
Corrections, 1992). Father neglect is abuse and quickly leads to
bullying, delinquency, drug abuse, teenage pregnancy, depression,
rebellion, and crime. News coverage of children exploding with
rage has become common. This epidemic of aggression and violence in the schoolyard is fueled by unresolved conflict at home.
Like a sleeping volcano, abuse and neglect at home will eventually erupt and injure innocent victims.

President Clinton recently announced that 6,093 students
were expelled for carrying firearms to school during the 1996-1997

school year. Nearly ten percent (10%) of these youngsters were elementary school students. Weapons carried to school are signs of anger, fear, and unresolved conflict. Countless children are lost, due to neglect, while others routinely experience abuse and violence. Like mirrors, children reflect their culture; they embrace the prevailing attitudes and values of their society.

Abuse is contagious. When children do not experience positive relationships at home, the negative debris is carried into subsequent relationships. Countless victims unknowingly pass painful memories, silent and unresolved, to their children. In the end, our communities pay dearly, both in terms of violence and suffering.

The reversal of this violent epidemic begins with parents. In a healthy (functional) family, children are the main concern. Parents break destructive (dysfunctional) patterns when they model respectful relationships. Fortunately, values learned at home effect children for the rest of their lives, including subsequent generations. As this happens, our community benefits.

Imprisoned fathers must learn to build promising relationships. But how will fathers who never knew their own father, learn to father their children? Only fathers can teach young men about the social roles of manhood and fatherhood. Incarcerated fathers have taught me that we must deal with past injuries before we tackle present relationships and future goals. Until Dad deals with his own pain, he cannot listen to the hurt of his child. As Dad deals with his demons, he is better able to become a father.

Over the next ten chapters, we will discuss the role of men in our society, the importance of accepting personal responsibility for our behavior, and the traits of a healthy father. We will talk about manhood because we must become men before we can become fathers. We will talk about relationships because they are vital to wholeness. We will discuss ways to interact with our children because they are life's central purpose. And finally, we will talk about our own experience, so we are not doomed to repeat it. Understanding our journey will give us valuable insight into the behavior of our children.

*Love is all we have, the only way
that each can help the other.*

–Euripides

QUESTION

*Behind the din of clanging doors,
Through the steel of fortress glass,
Under the glare of eternal lights,
Inside the curls of barbed wire,
Reside the fathers of two million
Children with wounds for souls.*

*The sky is dark;
The future is filled with violence!
Our blood will pay the debt
Of our insistence that we were right.*

*We say there are two classes of people,
The good and the evil.
The good are outside,
And the evil within.*

*But what if the system grows,
And the wire is strung like ribbons,
Who will be free and who imprisoned?*

–Wolfgang

ANDE –A True Story

It was our final class. As I passed out the class evaluations, students hunched over their desks to complete the form. The room grew quiet. I looked at each student with silent appreciation: Lenny, Mexico, Roberto, Warren, Sam, BJ, and John.... My heart swelled. I had seen changes in these men: Wesley, Williams, Dave, Cuba, Ryan, Shell, and Ande....

I recalled the morning Ande burst into my room, "This class is breaking me apart," he said. "For ten years I've lived in my cave, licking my wounds like a dog. I am becoming strong, so I will never be hurt again. I determined to use people before they used me."

I silently prayed that Ande would not drop the class. I could see the anguish on his face.

"Now I am learning..." Ande paused with a lump in his throat; tears collected along the bottom of his eyes. "...I'm learning that I've poisoned my heart. I've healed on the outside, but in here there is bitterness and poison." Ande moved his hands across his powerful chest.

Whew! The air went out of the room! Before me stood an intimidating, thirty-something man toughened by a decade at the penitentiary. His broad shoulders were stuffed into a green tee shirt, his slim waist surrounded by a wide, black weight-lifting belt.

"Mr. Wolfman, I have not written to my family or had any contact with them for over ten years. I got thirty years, I figured I would get five. You don't know what that did to me...thirty years."

Since joining my class, Ande has reestablished contact with Ashley, his daughter, and Doss, his nephew. How would I ever forget Ande's vulnerability and trust toward me? A prisoner guards the length of his sentence because "time" is a shameful secret. It is an honor when a man doing "heavy time" confesses the length of his sentence.

I was reading homework assignments one afternoon when Ande stopped by and softly asked, "Do you have a few minutes?"

When I nodded, he pulled the gray chair from behind a desk and whispered, "Someone is coming to see me whom I love very much." I strained to hear his soft words, "she hurt me." Ande's head dropped down to his chest heaving with sobs. He continued, "I don't know what to tell her. I love her, but I still have seventeen years. I can't ask her to wait seventeen years. I want to bless her and let her go. It's like a knife in my heart. Help me."

I never dreamed of encountering this depth of tenderness in prison. There is nothing so sacred and painful as watching someone in deep anguish.

In the following weeks Ande contacted his family, and Doss came to visit. Ande told me that his nephew talked of revenge. At that point, Ande held up his hand and said, "Look at you, a big, handsome man. I don't want you to settle any score for me. I want you to find your own happiness."

Mexico stood up, interrupting my reflection and bringing me back to our final class. He began speaking in Spanish to Señor Roberto. Although I could not understand his words, I could feel his passion. When Mexico sat down, Roberto spoke.

"Mr. Wolfgang, Mexico wants to thank you for the class. Before he came to prison, he was the manager of sixty employees. When Mexico was arrested, he was training to become the manager of 160 workers. So much responsibility has made Mexico reflective and quiet. Even elders in the community depended on Mexico for work and talked to him about their problems. When Mexico signed up for this class, he didn't expect to learn anything; he wanted to watch the videos and pass time. Now, he says this is one of the best classes he ever had. He talks to his daughters about their feelings, something he never did before. He wants you to know that even though he was quiet in class, he learned very much."

Sam interrupted with his Jamaican accent, "Teacher, Mexico is changed. We talk. Mexico used to be inside himself, troubled about his family. His wife remarried and lives in New York; he wonders if he will ever see his daughters again. When Mexico is released, INS (Immigration and Naturalization Service) will deport him to Mexico. But Mexico is not inside himself anymore. He believes it will somehow work that he will be able to see his family."

Ande stood and surprised me with his words, "Now we tell about the Wolfman."

Uh oh! I felt a knot of apprehension as gentle laughter bubbled around the room.

"The Wolfman comes to us as a child; he doesn't have anything to hide. We come to class filled with bitterness and rage. The Wolfman just looks at us with interest and hears us."

Ande had taken that first step to open his heart, not only to me, but also to other inmates. Prisoners rarely open their hearts to the other men. In prison, information is power. Ande continued, "I run and exercise like a madman, trying to make myself strong, so no one ever takes advantage of me again. But this Wolfman shows me that healing doesn't begin on the outside, it starts in here." Ande jabbed himself in the chest.

"The Wolfman is sincere, so when we pretend to be macho, he just watches, and we soon realize that we are acting foolishly."

Ande had broken the ice. One by one, the men spoke of their appreciation for the class and me. I squeezed my eyes together, but no matter, hot tears flowed down my face. I felt my heart expanding to receive their gratitude. I will never forget how the men affirmed me.

Dear Wolfman,

You are a blessed man, my precious friend.
Indeed, you are a healer, the wizard of emotion
Because in your tears is a loving magic
That whoever is touched by it,
No one could possibly be the same.
You awaken in men the dormant
Spirit of his beauty and respect.
You are the mirror of our souls,
And your tears and our tears
Are the blessed water
That calms our pain and purifies our Spirit.
You mirror our own love, pain, and compassion,
So through them, we can have a clear understanding
That we are the precious, playful, and unique children
    of creation.
Love has no boundaries;

It has the power that makes us endure this adventure;
It leads us to our Promised Land.

–Ande

Healing comes when authentic men and women cast aside indifference, risk themselves, and care about each other. I want you to meet some of the students from my classes and know them as men instead of prisoners. In their world of bitterness, revenge, and greed, these men never learned about intimacy or empathy. I watch them walk into my first class as tough, bitter, and alienated men. Six months later they leave with new understanding and respect. Healing is about acceptance, group support, accountability, and understanding. These men never had a father to teach them about manhood, much less fatherhood.

Dr. Karl Menninger says, "Prison need not be the end of the road but the beginning of an interesting and productive life."

I hope you will join me as we explore fatherhood.

ANDE

Ande: *A man with pain in his eyes*
Ande: *A prisoner worn with time*
Ande: *A soul that dares to dream*
Ande: *A spirit reaching for life*
Ande: *A courage that refuses to be torn*
Ande laughing, "There's laughter under the suffering."

–Wolfgang

Chapter 1

TRUST

Before a baby can understand love, he must feel warm and safe. Security creates trust. Trust is the foundation of a good relationship and the beginning of intimacy. Trust is the willingness to open our heart to others, daring to risk and show concern. Mutual trust brings feelings of security, warmth, and respect. In turn, this creates a solid foundation, which builds intimacy.

Tough attitudes: "I don't care," or "I'll show you," are signs of broken trust. Even "love," one of our favorite words, has become superficial because many of us have been deeply "burnt" by broken promises. It is very difficult to love someone we cannot trust. Love without trust is disappointing...and painful!

Jeff told Tammy that she was beautiful and he loved her. Three weeks later Tammy came home from work a little early and caught Jeff with his arms around Debbie. Tammy exploded. If Jeff wants Tammy to love him, he had better stop playing around and breaking his promises. Broken promises destroy trust.

Families teach children to trust. Eric Erikson, the developmental psychologist, teaches us that a child unconsciously learns "basic trust" during the first year of life. Basic trust comes from responsible, sensitive, and dependable care. Mistrust follows neglect and abuse. When our family violates our trust, it scars us for life then spills over to our children. Dad destroys Mom's confidence by walking out. Mom injures Dad by not telling him the whole story. Parents destroy the trust of a child through deceit and abuse. Neglect, a silent type of abuse, quietly destroys our ability for meaningful relationships although we may never realize the extent of the damage.

When I asked my prison class to deal with painful memories of broken trust, Jim reached down deep and wrote this letter:

Dear Mom,

I hold a lot of resentment toward you. All I ever wanted was a normal family. You were either too sick or too drunk to see the needs of your children. In second grade, even though the school was nearby, I wasn't allowed to come home during lunch. That hurt! One day I took the house key and came home knowing that you would be in bed nursing your hangover. Instead, I saw you on the sofa with a stranger. In that instant, Mom, my dream of a normal family died. From that day until now, it has been impossible for me to trust women. I blew a perfectly wonderful marriage to a beautiful lady because of my paranoia and accusations. I used to call LaRee three times a day and accuse her of things I now know only you could do. I drove her away, Mom, and in the process I hurt my children and myself. I love you, Mom.

Love, Jim

Jim was deeply wounded because the mother/child relationship is so very important. Primary relationships such as mother/child, father/child, and husband/wife cause more suffering than casual friendships. Deep emotional injuries can hurt forever. Jim's relationship with LaRee failed because of the unresolved fear and hurt carried from childhood. Trust broken during childhood will damage future relationships.

Fathers complete the circle of trust. Webster's Dictionary defines trust as: "a firm belief...in the honesty, integrity, reliability, justice, et cetera, of another person or thing; faith; reliance."

Dad, your love and faithfulness are needed in the family. In healthy families, trust deepens as the family spends time together and affirms one another during crisis.

JOEL

Dee interrupted the class to say, "I lie to my son Joel. Lying will make him strong. If you don't lie to your child, he becomes weak and the strong will use him. I'm teaching my son to be tough."

Children, like Joel, who live with deceit also live in fear. Yes, they may become tough and cynical, but lies destroy their ability for intimacy and positive relationships. Dee is naïve, lying to Joel will drive a wedge of suspicion and bitterness between Dee and his son that will not soon be forgiven—or forgotten. Joel holds people at a distance because he assumes everyone is like his father, out to take advantage of him. Children who live with deceit and abuse withdraw deep inside themselves to avoid being hurt. They turn the lies and hurt into indifference and bitterness. You can hear it in their words, "Who cares?" Or, "I don't give a d—." Indifference is not only a wounded cry for understanding, but also an attempt to stay numb and not feel the pain.

Abuse is a gross violation of trust. Neglect, verbal abuse, physical abuse, and sexual abuse destroy human dignity. We now know that perpetrators of abuse are prior victims. Children of abuse do not experience unconditional love. Instead, they mistake the pleasurable feelings of puppy love and sexual arousal for true love and intimacy. How can a child unfamiliar with genuine love but familiar with neglect and abuse commit to a family?

BARRIERS

It is natural to pull back from pain and abuse. Withdrawal creates a gap that protects us from emotional hurt and suffering. But we must realize that withdrawal also creates barriers to intimacy and wholeness. The barriers that we build to keep other people out, lock us in. Joel withdraws from Dee into the silent resentment of his own jail. The thicker that Joel builds his emotional jail, the more difficult it will be for him to break out and find relational intimacy. Joel is following the detached pattern of his father although he promised, "I will never be like my dad." How will Joel learn to trust? How will he learn to be honest when his own father treats him dishonestly? In the end, the walls of silence that we build to protect us, isolate us from intimacy that we desperately need.

We are all children of trust and mistrust (fear). We begin to destroy the barriers when we create a climate of trust where people can honestly express themselves. Trust and honest communication are the secret of warm, meaningful friendships. On the other hand, the climate of mistrust: lies, threats, and broken promises, leads to fear and subsequent violence. Without trust, love is empty and painful, frequently ending in abuse.

Jail is a hotbed of fear and mistrust. With recidivism above sixty percent (60%), it is obvious that fear and punishment do not rehabilitate. Bullying behavior is a direct result of broken trust, unresolved fear, and anger. Until we teach the bully how to become relational, instead of aggressive and passive, society will suffer.

Fathers must build and rebuild foundations of trust for their families. We must stop lying to ourselves about how wonderful we are as fathers and attempt to see life from the eyes of our children. We must make and keep our promises, so our children will grow strong. Responsible parents build healthy families.

HURT

May, 1998

Dear Dad,

It will seem strange for you to get a letter from me to talk about something that has been buried for fifteen years. It's not gone, Dad, just hidden under layers of anger and bitterness. I'm talking about the time you violated my trust. How dare you! I withdrew from you and I have been withdrawing from myself ever since. Long ago my laugh became empty, my heart lost its song, and I became obsessed with control. I remember you tried to "fix" me by buying me junk when I needed you to apologize and ask forgiveness. I am tired of carrying around this poison, and it's time I learn to trust myself again. I go to therapy, and until I get this out, I will not heal. I am sorry we didn't know how to deal with this.

Love, Sara

Sara experienced sexual abuse, and now she lives with a wound that refuses to heal. Sara wants to find peace; her father needs the same peace. However, neither knows how to begin the process of healing. When trust is destroyed, the relationship suffers until safety is reestablished. Sara cannot get rid of her bitterness and anger until she confronts her father with the betrayal. This will take time and honest communication.

Dad also lives in brokenness because he failed to protect Sara. Shame and guilt, perhaps unconscious, will affect his health and emotional balance. Of course, Dad is the offender; he will live with the consequences of his behavior and try to cover his shame, possibly with an addiction like alcoholism. Dad needs attention and reconciliation as desperately as Sara.

HEALING

The only cure for this relationship is to confess the hurt and confront the shame and anger. Until Dad and Sara are willing to deal with this deep pain, the wound will not heal. Sara has taken the first step by confronting her father. He can help her heal by accepting responsibility for the abuse.

Sara's hurt affects her other relationships. Even now Sara is on guard when reaching for acceptance and love. Fear is a natural consequence of the disrespect shown by her father. Once we fall through the thin ice into cold water, we never forget. It will take a relationship as significant as Sara's relationship with her father to repair her injury. In other words, the depth of the wound must be the depth of the repair. This is the secret of relational therapy. Sara must confront her memories and fear, to discover that level of intimacy.

INTIMACY

If we think about it, the level of trust in a relationship is the level of intimacy. This is important because it means that if we desire more closeness, we must deepen trust. We do this by behaving responsibly and respectfully.

Dad, your son needs a trusting relationship, or he will grow to become a fragile man, unable to commit to his own family because no one committed to him. Your daughter needs a trusting relationship, or she may never grow to trust another man, and her children will unconsciously reap her pain. Broken father/child relationships violate the child and create barriers that lead to dysfunctional (unhealthy) behavior such as neglect, depression, abuse, and violence. Dedicated fathers create a trusting father/child relationship that helps the child feel safe and warm. There is no reason for a secure child to erect barriers that isolate her from intimacy and love.

TELLING YOUR CHILD

Incarcerated fathers ask me, "What do I tell my child about being in jail?"

This is a very difficult question; fathers do not want their children to carry the burden of incarceration.

Luis told his daughter Ruth Anne that he was working in Pennsylvania. When Ruthie would ask Dad to come home, Luis would say, "I'm working so I can buy you nice toys and clothes."

When Ruthie visited her father to celebrate her fourth birthday, her first words were, "Daddy, I don't want no more toys. I just want you to come home with me." Luis barely caught his breath before she continued, "And why are the policemen always here?"

Luis confessed that the words cut his heart like a knife. "Come here, girl, we need to talk."

It is obvious that little Ruth Anne has been thinking about her father's absence. It is remarkable that this young child has enough courage to confront her father with the truth.

If you expect your child to trust you, there will come a moment when you must be honest. This will take courage and timing. What you say depends on her age and understanding. If your child hears the truth from you, she will trust you. If your child hears the truth from someone else, and you refuse to talk about your incarceration, your child will feel shunned and unimportant. She may not have the courage to confront you, and the secret will become a barrier.

Little children who abruptly lose their fathers will feel abandoned. Remaining family members can help the child deal with this "thin ice" feeling by making him feel safe and secure. Offer the child opportunities to express his sadness and fear because Daddy left home so suddenly. The child may need reassurance that Mommy will not leave. Plan to visit Dad, so the child can be reassured of his love. Avoid changes that threaten the child until he begins to feel safe again. For example, avoid leaving the child with a strange babysitter, leaving him alone for extended periods of time, or putting him in fearful situations.

Elementary age children may think that your incarceration is their fault, "Daddy left me and Mommy 'cause I was bad." Respect your child enough to talk with her about the situation. Young children will want to know, "What about me?" Or, "When are you coming home?" They need information about how this will affect their lives and reassurance that you care for them. Explain in language that they can understand; children do not understand time the way we do as adults. "Not for a long, long time, Ruthie, you will be fourteen years old when I come home. That makes me very sad. I will write to you and think of you every day because I love you so much. You make me happy."

I encourage you to hold and hug your child when you talk. She needs this reassurance of your love.

The relationship between Luis and Ruth Anne healed when Luis found the courage to break the ice and be honest. Now they can talk about other deep issues because they stopped pretending and dared to confront the pain inside. Do not pretend; it destroys trust. Play it straight up. When I asked Luis how it went with Ruthie, he smiled broadly and said, "Aww, man, forget about it. It's there—if you know what I mean."

Teenagers deserve honesty. When you talk with your teenager, she might ask you questions such as, "How do I deal with teachers and friends who don't know where you are?"

Esther was in fifth grade when Mr. Weitzel talked about vocations. Esther did not want to talk about her father because he was in prison. When Mr. Weitzel looked at Esther, she told the class that her mother worked at Stone Creek Inn. June started laughing, and when Mr. Weitzel asked June what was funny, she blurted, "Esther's daddy's in jail." The class snickered as Esther's face began to bum; then she started to cry.

Families need to talk about awkward situations that children like Esther will encounter, and agree on solutions. Of course, this is not possible if Dad is pretending to be at college. Do not play Russian roulette with your child's feelings; someday the truth will surface. Communication builds trust and intimacy. This is a wonderful opportunity to talk about a difficult issue and grow together—a teaching moment.

One final note, to be a responsible father, if you never had one, may create a feeling of resentment. After all, you are giving your child something you never had the privilege to receive. Absent fathers do not help their children learn about community. In fact, they injure community by not providing a positive male role. How will a son who has never been fathered, learn to father his children? Fatherhood is a role taught by responsible fathers. If you never had a father, you can surrender to the resentment by neglecting your children, or you can heal the wound by involving yourself in their lives.

AUTOBIOGRAPHY IN FIVE SHORT CHAPTERS

Chapter I.
I walk down the street.
There is a deep hole in the sidewalk.
I fall in.
I am lost...I am helpless.
It isn't my fault.
It takes forever to find a way out.

Chapter II.
I walk down the same street.
There is a deep hole in the sidewalk.
I pretend I don't see it.
I fall in again.
I can't believe I am in the same place.
But, it isn't my fault.
It still takes a long time to get out.

Chapter III.
I walk down the same street.
There is a deep hole in the sidewalk.
I see it is there.
I still fall in ... it's a habit.
My eyes are open.
I know where I am.
It is my fault.
I get out immediately.

Chapter IV.
I walk down the same street.
There is a deep hole in the sidewalk.
I walk around it.

Chapter V.
I walk down another street.

—Portia Nelson

As the author suggests, behavior begins to change when we accept responsibility for our choices.

Trust is vital to family and community wholeness. Trust takes time, commitment, integrity, and communication. Trust brings intimacy; intimacy brings healing.

"There's nothing wrong with having been a criminal. There is something wrong with remaining a criminal."

—Malcolm X

Chapter 2

AWARENESS

"I put all my time and energy into taking care of others. I never talked with people about my own life, so no one could see me, nor could I see myself. I understood what every one else was going through but not me. I assumed I was the savior of the world, but I wouldn't talk about me...my pain, fear, emotions, desires, or past events. I could only teach what I'd been taught and give what I had been given. My inner self was hidden away, mostly from me. I didn't trust anyone with my secrets, my sin, and my shame. I didn't trust myself. I trusted others to know me better than myself. Now I am learning the greatest adventure of life is me. I must learn to know me."

—Guru

FACES

Buried deep in our memories are secrets of childhood that we hide, mostly from ourselves, because they are too painful to recollect. Names such as stupid, fatso, ugly, sissy, lazy, and dummy make us feel angry and ashamed, so we withdraw and put on a mask. This "face" protects our fragile but lost inner child and becomes an "inauthentic me."

Incarcerated men wear faces to hide their feelings. Some wear a tough mask to hide fear and pain. Others put on a happy face and "shoot the bull" about the "good old days," but inside they are depressed because of the long sentence, the boredom, and the loss of family. The only face we never dare wear is the "genuine me." This is especially true for men because they focus outwardly instead of inwardly on feelings. We cope by convincing ourselves that all is fine, even as the "genuine me" is lost to our memory.

Guru is tired of pretending and unhappy about not knowing himself. He is waking up to his own silence and uncovering his inner hurt and shame. This takes tremendous courage, but it is the only way to rediscover the beautiful person buried within.

The inner person is a child—feeling and fearful. Tenderness and acceptance are keys to healing this inner soul. Tenderness toward the inner self allows a father to be tender with his child. Until Dad deals with his own hurt and sorrow, how can he understand his child's pain?

Once we become aware of our inner child, everything changes. Opening the heart to feel anger, and more importantly, the pain and sorrow buried under the anger, is the path to discovering the forgotten self.

> **Who looks outside dreams—**
> **Who looks inside wakes.**
>
> **–Carl Jung**

STEVE

Steve sat in the back of the class with a numb look as I talked about the faces and masks we all wear. He finally spoke, "I don't know what you're talking about. I'm tough; that's just who I am. There is no little Stevie buried inside of me. There's nothing. I'm empty inside. All this business about being hurt inside and wearing a face, what are you talking about?"

Steve stayed after class, which was the beginning of our relationship. Over the weeks, I learned about his family and the apple of his eye, his beautiful daughter.

Something began to happen in Steve; I could feel it when we talked. However, this did not prepare me for his class confession. Steve stood up, took a deep breath, and looked around at the men. In his husky voice he began, "I've been learning about myself. At night when it's dark, I lay on my bunk and think about my childhood. This is new to me, I never allowed myself to feel pain. This week I went to bed and wrapped my arms around myself."

Steve paused and wrapped his big arms around his chest as the class chuckled nervously. Steve had been so cynical that we all wondered, "Is Steve being real?"

"When I was a child, I never got much love," he said. "Now I realize that I am hungry for love and affection. By the way, we don't get that here." The men snickered. "I didn't know he was in here, but lately I've been talking to little Stevie and helping him realize that all the pain in his life isn't his fault. My mom tried to commit suicide, and I found her; I was eight years old."

Steve's voice began to soften, and I could feel his hurt. "I plan to hug myself more often. I just wish I could hug my daughter."

When Steve finished, the class sat in warm, holy silence. We could feel the peace that Steve was discovering. These men acted like friends, not felons. The cold, clear night was beautiful.

Steve changed. Men who avoided Steve began to talk with him about their families. Instead of sitting alone in the back of the classroom, Steve slowly became a part of the circle even though he pushed his chair back a little.

I had an opportunity to meet Steve's brother, wife, and daughter in the visiting room. Steve hugged his beautiful daughter, and she fell asleep in his arms. Steve's ability to hug his daughter intimately was the consequence of him learning to hug himself.

Steve and Guru are waking up to the forgotten past. Until we awaken within, we cannot be open with others. When I feel my own pain, I begin to understand that we are reflections of each other. Time becomes precious as we accept our shame and allow it to transform us into compassionate men of healing.

STEPS TO EMOTIONAL WHOLENESS: H-E-A-L

Halt and heal the denial; stop feeling self-pity.
Express your emotions, especially anger, hurt, and fear.
Accept accountability for your life; stop blaming.
Love. Develop relationships of care; show concern.

WASHINGTON

During my last session at a nearby state prison, I asked the men if they wanted to share something that they had learned. In the rear, left corner of the room, Washington raised his hand. He said, "Mr. Wolfgang, I would like to thank you for this class. I learned a lot about my daughter and myself. I'm a lifer, and this class has helped me better understand my role as a father."

The word lifer caught my attention, so I inquired, "May I ask how long you have been incarcerated?"

"Since 1975," he replied.

I felt numb. In 1975 when I started college, Washington started life in a penitentiary. He would spend his entire life on a few acres of prison soil.

"I have one daughter, she is now a mother. I am learning how to communicate with her. She was a baby when I left home."

Ouch! Words fail to express the deep grief of loss.

"What have you done to help pass your time?" I asked.

"I sign up for all the programs I can. I finished college, and I work in the chapel. I am doing all I can to understand myself and my world." Then with a smile Washington added, "I am enjoying getting to know my daughter."

Mr. Washington's humility touched me. I dare say, here was a man awakening to the person within, to his daughter, and to the world because of his inner journey to the self.

SELF

Self is everywhere shining forth from all beings, vaster than the vast, subtler than the most subtle, unreachable, yet nearer than breath, than heartbeat.

Eye cannot see it, ear cannot hear it nor tongue utter it; only in deep absorption can the mind, grown pure and silent, merge with the formless truth.

As soon as you find it, you are free; you have found yourself; you have solved the great riddle; your heart forever is at peace.

Whole, you enter the Whole. Your personal self returns to its radiant, intimate, deathless source.

—Upanishad

AWARENESS

Self-awareness is the beginning of wisdom. Until I understand my nature, how can I understand the nature of our world?

We can divide a person into two hemispheres: the lower self, and the higher self. Even the word "individual" appears to be a compound of indivisible and dual, which shows us the indivisible duality of our lower and higher natures. Sigmund Freud referred to the lower self as the id (German "it"). This is the natural, physical, and earthly body that develops according to the genetic code (DNA) deeply buried in our cells. Unconsciously, our bodies develop and grow according to biological blueprints; no one thinks about breathing or digesting food. Instinctively, babies cry when they are hungry or hurt. Our lower self is unconscious and impulsive, like a child throwing a temper tantrum. The child is not controlled by reason but driven by inner passions. The lower self is passionate, untamed, and demanding.

HIGHER SELF

As we learn and grow, social interaction begins to influence our childish behavior. This awareness, or consciousness, is the higher self. This consciousness is different from our lower "animal" (id) nature. Animals do not have the ability to reflect. Freud referred to this higher reasonable self as the ego, which develops through reflection and relationship. As men and women learn to understand themselves and respect the boundaries of others, we become conscious (aware). The ego (adult self), although pulled by our unconscious id (passions) finds freedom in awareness. Now that we are conscious of our own behavior, we begin to learn from others.

Together our higher and lower natures complete the person. Our lower self reminds us of our physical need for food, safety, rest, sex, avoidance of pain, warmth, et cetera. The id also triggers our fear, which alerts us to danger.

It is important for the higher self to plan opportunities for fun and refreshment that responsibly vent the desires of the lower self. New Year's, Mardi Gras, July 4th, vacation, and even Friday evening are times when we allow ourselves to enjoy passion and adventure. Although we can repress (cage) the id for a time, if we ignore our lower nature for too long, the id will break free...imagine a cooped in, ten-year-old boy. Athletics, exercise, music, dance, intimacy, relationships, and recreation are possible ways to unwind the lower self. Plan activities to express passion and energy appropriately.

Our higher self builds community and protects the earth. Men who injure society have not developed their higher nature. Buddha teaches that suffering and pain can lead to this higher path of consciousness. Once we have felt the sting of suffering, we do not want others to endure the same. Incarcerated men often tell me, "I wouldn't wish this on my worst enemy."

UNIVERSAL SELF

Beyond our individual higher and lower natures, lies the gateway of the universal Self. In other words, without even realizing it, we are blossoms on the universal tree; creation has placed us here. Together we are reflections of the collective awareness: Self–capital "S." Once this understanding penetrates our higher self, it breeds a newfound spirit of respect for the dignity and beauty of all creation.

RESPECT

I live along a country road where people tend to throw garbage. One day as Andi and I were picking up another box of empty beer bottles, she asked, "Dad, why do you pick up this stuff? Tomorrow someone will come along and dump more trash."

I did not know what to say. I asked Andi to let me think about it.

I shared her question with my class because I learn so much from my students. Mike Chan said, "Mr. Wolfgang, tell your daughter that you respect the earth because you respect yourself. When we learn to respect ourselves, we respect all of life."

What a beautiful insight! Human beings are the conscious guardians of the earth; we can destroy her or heal her. Our reckless pollution of the sky, water, soil, and life is ignorant and destructive, contrary to the purpose of creation. Awareness of our higher nature brings us into harmony with creation.

Society must be built on this balance of respect and consciousness for all. Citizens establish collective principles of
respect and fairness, otherwise known as government. When our
government acts responsibly, the community prospers. When the
system acts irresponsibly, trust erodes and people resort to their
own brand of justice. This leads to anarchy and chaos, where the
bully with the biggest weapon wins. We must coestablish rules of
respect that challenge us to set aside our prejudice and build
communities of equality and justice.

CONSCIOUSNESS

Families are the best place for children to learn consciousness.
As families practice mutual respect, children learn appropriate
interaction. On the other hand, neglect encourages a child to
meet her needs through impulsive and demanding behavior.

So you see, fatherhood is not about making babies or being
the boss. Instead, fatherhood is about becoming conscious of our
responsibility to family and community. Fathers must become
men before they can become fathers. Men unaware of their
social responsibility sleep in the unconscious self. They blame
the system for failing to meet their needs and desires. Mature
men accept responsibility for the impulsive lower self. They
embrace the challenge of fatherhood and social responsibility
even as they reach for universal awareness.

DON'T BE FOOLED BY ME

Don't be fooled by me.
Don't be fooled by the face I wear.
For I wear a thousand masks—
Masks that I am afraid to take off,
And none of them are me.
Pretending is an art
That's second nature with me,
But don't be fooled—

I give the impression that I'm secure,
Within as well as without,
That confidence is my name

And coolness my game,
That the water's calm
And I'm in command,
And that I need no one.
But don't believe me. Please.
Beneath dwells the real me
In confusion, in fear, and aloneness.
But I hide this.
I panic at the thought of my weakness
And fear of being exposed.
That's why I frantically create
A mask to hide behind—
To help me pretend, to shield me
From the glance that knows.
But such a glance is my salvation.
That is, if it's followed by acceptance,
If it's followed by love.
It's the only thing that will assure me
Of what I can't assure myself:
That I'm worth something.

But I don't tell you this.
I don't dare.
I'm afraid your glance will not be
Followed by acceptance and love.
I'm afraid you'll think less of me,
That you'll laugh at me—
I'm afraid that deep down I'm nothing,
That I'm no good
And that you will see this and reject me.

So I play my game, my desperate game.
I idly chatter to you
In the suave tones of surface talk.
I tell you everything that is really nothing,
And nothing of what's everything,
Of what's crying within me.

So, don't be fooled by what I'm saying.
Please listen carefully
And try to hear what I am not saying,

What I'd like to be able to say,
What, for survival, I need to say.
I dislike hiding. Honestly!
I really want to be genuine
And spontaneous—and ME.
You can help me.
You can hold out your hand,
Even when that's the last thing
I seem to want.
You can wipe away from my eyes
The blank stare of living death.
You can call me into aliveness.
Each time you're kind, and gentle,
And encouraging,
Each time you try to understand
Because you really care,
My heart begins to grow wings.
With your sensitivity and sympathy
And your power of understanding,
You breathe life into me.
I want you to know that.

I want you to know
How important you are to me.
You can break down the walls
Behind which I tremble.
You can help me remove my masks.
A long conviction of worthlessness
Builds strong walls
But I am told—
That love is stronger than walls,
And in this lies my hope.
Please help me beat down those walls
With firms hands, but gentle hands—
For the child inside is very sensitive.
Who am I, you may wonder?
I am someone you know very well.
For I am every man you meet
And every woman you meet.

–Peter Lehman

Chapter 3

LIFESTYLE

Laura values trust, integrity, and friendship. Her motto is, "When it's loving, it's right."

Gus values image, money, and pleasure. His motto is, "Image is everything."

Based on this information, tell me...
- Who owns a sleek, black Mercedes?
- Who volunteers in prison?
- Who dreams of buying a condo in West Palm Beach?
- Who spends weekends with children and family?

Our lifestyle is shaped by our values. Values are the important and meaningful priorities of life. Just as the Rocky Mountains and Pacific Ocean effect the climate pattern of the Western Hemisphere, so values determine our attitudes and behavior, yet we are mostly unaware of their influence. Early on I accepted the political tradition of my family; now, I vote my political conscience. I moved to the mountains because I value solitude. If I value family, I act responsibly toward my wife and children. If I value basketball, it becomes a part of my life. Men are taught to value sports but not tenderness. Personally, I value intimacy, honesty, blueberry pie, understanding, Italian cuisine, and vacations with close friends.

There are universal values, national values, traditional values, economic values, educational values, social values, spiritual values, and even criminal values. Universal values are important to all people: peace, freedom, family, recreation, love, education, faith, et cetera. National values include patriotism, honor, achievement, and courage. Love, family ties, faith, morality, and truthfulness are considered traditional values. Criminal values include power, control, deception, toughness, pleasure, and manipulation.

Children naturally accept the values of those closest to them: family, friends, and neighborhood. They are too naïve to question the patterns that shape their personality. Parents teach integrity and truth by living honestly. We teach respect by being kind. We teach patience by being tolerant. When we ask, "How did you do on your math test?" we teach the value of listening. This is why it is so very important to interact with children:

"Do you prefer the red jacket or the blue one?"

"What do you think about this?"

Respect children enough to ask for their ideas and opinions. They learn respect when they are respected.

CHILDREN LEARN WHAT THEY LIVE

If children live with criticism, they learn to condemn.
If children live with hostility, they learn to fight.
If children live with fear, they learn to be apprehensive.
If children live with pity, they learn to feel sorry for themselves.
If children live with ridicule, they learn to be shy.
If children live with jealousy, they learn what envy is.
If children live with shame, they learn to feel guilty.
If children live with tolerance, they learn to be patient.
If children live with encouragement, they learn to be confident.
If children live with praise, they learn to appreciate.
If children live with approval, they learn to like themselves.
If children live with acceptance, they learn to find love in the world.
If children live with recognition, they learn to have a goal.
If children live with sharing, they learn to be generous.
If children live with honesty and fairness, they learn what
*   truth and justice are.*
If children live with security, they learn to have faith in
*   themselves and in those around them.*
If children live with friendliness, they learn that the world
*   is a nice place in which to live.*
If children live with serenity, they learn to have peace of mind.
With what are your children living?

–Dorothy L. Nolte

Not all lifestyles are positive. Father neglect fails to teach young men how to assume social and family responsibility. Charles was four the first time he hit his father for trying to drown his mother in the bathtub. His father threw him down the steps. Lifestyles of deceit, abuse, and greed do not teach children the value of respect, empathy, and commitment.

> **Values are the prison from which children rebel,**
> **The law from which they live,**
> **Or the nest from which they fly.**
>
> **–Wolfgang**

The media: television, music, video, and the Internet increasingly influence the values of our society. Media art and language are designed to grab our attention and seduce us to consumerism. Please understand the influence of the media, and limit your child's access to destructive values.

RYAN

Ryan was put out on the street when he was six years old because his stepfather believed he was a demon. Ryan remembers his fear and the hurt of never seeing his mother. He moved from one foster home to another until he was old enough to hang out on the corner with guys who paid him to run errands. Now Ryan is forty-two years old and has spent twenty years behind bars. He is just completing a sentence for armed robbery. Sure, Ryan is responsible for his choices. But we must also agree that Ryan is a victim. He chose a lifestyle that helped him deal with the street. Twenty years in prison have also shaped his life. The values we embrace are seeds, or perhaps weeds, planted deeply before we are conscious of their impact.

I remind parents, "Know your child's friends." Why? Because as Ronald Johnson says, "If you play in the mud, you're gonna get dirty. If you stand in the rain, you're gonna get wet. If you run with dogs, you're gonna catch fleas."

Suppose your children follow your values and lifestyle? If we hope to change our children, we must change ourselves. We are not damned to walk blindly in the same rut. Mahatma Gandhi, Nelson Mandella, and Martin Luther King, Jr. each chose paths to improve the social, economic, and spiritual well-being of their community. Martin Luther King, Jr. set out to make a difference in Montgomery, Alabama, and ended up challenging the world.

Men, we have an opportunity to make a difference. Start by communicating with your children, this is the greatest achievement. Too many prisoners waste their unique ability by hanging out on the block month after month. You are priceless and unique. Dedicate yourself to learn and grow.

DON'T BE AFRAID TO FAIL

You've failed many times, although you may not remember.
You fell down the first time you tried to walk.
You almost drowned the first time you tried to swim,
  didn't you?
Did you hit the ball the first time you swung a bat?
Heavy hitters, the ones who hit the most home runs,
  also strike out a lot.
R.H. Macy failed seven times before his store in New York
  caught on.
English novelist John Creasey got 753 rejection slips before
  he published 564 books.
Babe Ruth struck out 1,330 times, but he also hit 714 runs.
Don't worry about failure.
Worry about the chances you miss when you don't even try.

–Wall Street Journal
United Technologies Corporation
Hartford, Connecticut

JONAS

Jonas had bandwidth—a sign of intelligence. I was astonished to discover that Jonas had never finished high school and did not intend to sign up for the G.E.D. program. I wondered, "How can this man neglect such obvious ability?"

I said, "Jonas, you seem to have potential and intelligence. Are you going to take some classes or just put in time?"

During the past two years, Jonas finished the Parenting class, completed his G.E.D., and received certificates for horticulture, heating and air-conditioning, and carpentry. The last time we talked, he was enrolled in college accounting.

Of course, I would like to take credit for Jonas's decision to increase his options, but I suspect the real reason he went back to school is because his best friend, Martin, encouraged him. By attending classes together, Martin helped change his friend's life.

WEALTH

Education is a precious value. A century ago, most of us would have been fortunate to complete high school. We would have worked alongside our father and learned his trade, just as he learned it from his father. Public education changed all of that and offered us the opportunity to earn an education. We live during an exceptional time.

But there is change on the horizon. Technology is changing our cultural patterns and increasing society's demand for specialized employees. Think of it this way; until about 1950, a student would have studied the same subjects that his mother and grandfather studied. Today, textbooks may be outdated in a few years. As the cost of education continues to spiral upward, the window of opportunity will narrow. In the meantime, it is important to develop our minds and challenge our children to learn about matters that will influence the 21st century.

Does this mean that we must be a whiz kid to succeed? Definitely not! But it is obvious that the better paying jobs will belong to skilled persons who have developed their ability through vocational schools and college programs. Unskilled laborers will be plentiful and poorly paid.

Wealth is not just about money; people with options are wealthy. They can choose where they live and what they do with their time. Education increases our options and therefore, our wealth. It is important that we encourage our children to study. Challenge them to turn off the television and read a book. Offer your children incentives to read. How about finding the same book, possibly through an interlibrary loan, reading it together, and discussing the ideas?

40
ROWE

Rowe remained after class to talk about his ex-wife. We slipped into plastic chairs on either side of a brown table near the window covered with imposing gray bars. Like a shadow, steel and concrete denied our freedom.

"I am caught between two worlds, between the world of the mind and the world of the heart," Rowe said. "I never knew the world of the heart until I met Myra, my ex-wife. My father and mother were kind, but they worked all the time. When we talked, it was about our daily routines. We never shared our feelings and dreams. Until I got locked up, I was busy following the example of my parents, taking care of business. When Myra started sharing her feelings and was vulnerable, I didn't understand. I figured she was weak, and I turned on her in anger and ignorance. Prison has helped me to think about my life, and now I realize that Myra gave me a beautiful gift. I want to return her gift, but she's afraid to let me near her—I don't blame her, I used her."

I remember asking, "It sounds like you still love her?"

"I do."

Rowe looked deeply into my eyes then glanced away as his eyes turned glassy. I could not answer Rowe's question about Myra, but I said, "Rowe, you seem to be on a journey. I appreciate the courage it took for you to be so open with me. You have given me the beautiful gift of your confidence. As for Myra, I suggest that you follow your heart."

The buzzer rang to announce the ten-minute move. Rowe and I exchanged salutations before he headed out the door to his unit.

On Monday Rowe returned. "Mr. Wolfgang, I didn't sleep after we talked. I used to look in the window of your classroom and think you were a shallow teacher, stuffed with pompous answers. When we talked last Thursday, you helped me. I didn't sleep because I struggled with letting you into my drama. I've never let a white man into my drama before. I finally realized, either I allow you into my drama, or I continue to live with fear and prejudice."

THE DRAMA

Love so strong...seeping tears,
Feelings of hurt, resentment, and anger are real.
How can I repay all the years?
How will I ever forgive the knowledge to feel?
Words are useless, you see through deep shadows in my heart.
Make me see the truth beyond myself.
I strive to be a part
Of your drama: my existence.
You teach about soul and love within.
You live for others...it all makes sense.
Fear grips me, how will I be true?
It looks so effortless and natural,
Giving, loving, learning, teaching...hurting.
My highest hope is only to one day be like you.

–Angi Wolfgang

Rowe stuck out his hand for a handshake. "Welcome to my drama."

Rowe's beautiful spirit has taught me to question my own fear and prejudice. Mature men reserve the right to change their attitudes when confronted with new information. Relationships challenge our prejudice and invite us to lifestyles of integrity and understanding. I will always be indebted to Rowe.

THE RAFT

A man walking along a highroad sees a great river, its near bank dangerous and frightening, its far bank safe.

He collects sticks and foliage, makes a raft, paddles across the river and reaches the other shore.

Now suppose that, after he reaches the other shore, he takes the raft and puts it on his head wherever he goes. Would he be using the raft in an appropriate way?

No, a reasonable man will realize that the raft has been very useful to him in crossing the river and arriving safely on the other shore, but that once he has arrived, it is proper to leave the raft behind and walk on without it...

This is using the raft appropriately.

In the same way, all truths should be used to cross over; they should not be held on to once you have arrived. You should let go of even the most profound insight or the most wholesome teaching, all the more so, unwholesome teachings.

–The Buddha

CULTURE

Our values and lifestyle are a reflection of culture. Oh, we may talk about personal values, family values, traditional values, economic values, contemporary values, et cetera, but life is really a reflection of our cultural values. I enjoy mechanics, speak English, and play basketball because of my culture. Even our manners evolve according to tested patterns of culture and dissolve when cultural attitudes change. Families pass culture onto children. Our values of language, customs, holidays, diet, dreams, and attitudes are influenced by cultural traditions.

The United States is home to many ethnic groups and a broad array of different cultures. My mother grew up in West Virginia and my father is from Central Pennsylvania's coal region. I lived the best part of my childhood in Jamaica, where I enjoyed curry rice, dried fish, and swimming in the Caribbean. I experienced three cultures by the time I was eight years of age.

Behavior is not a result of race or color, as many naïve people suggest, but a consequence of culture. Studies indicate that even psychotic patients operate according to cultural patterns. For instance, in Western cultures, psychotic patients are often noisy. Our word bedlam actually comes from the hospital of St. Mary of Bethlehem, London, an insane asylum. In the Orient, psychotic patients are more docile.

Civilization is the collection of many cultures sharing common values: warmth, safety, recreation, work, children, love, freedom, laughter, achievement, fine food, et cetera. As our world grows smaller, dominant cultures threaten more fragile ones. As an example, European culture destroyed certain native Indian cultures. We must learn to appreciate the uniqueness and beauty of each culture; this inspires cultural unity, cultural beauty, and societal peace.

Negative lifestyles that include prejudice, greed, manipulation, and aggression threaten our neighborhoods and scare away families. Ignoring negative lifestyles undermines the security of the community. We need to question any prejudice that threatens freedom and life. Communities must deal responsibly and fairly with crime if we hope to live in peace.

In the midst of winter, I found there was within me, an invincible summer.

–Albert Camus

Dale said, "Mr. Wolfman, this is my third bit. If I don't pull it together, the next time I go down, they will throw away the key."

Dale is realizing that he must change his values before he can change his lifestyle. Values precede lifestyle.

There are internal and external values. Internal values are deeply planted in the core of our being. These are the principles that govern our life. That is to say, a person might refuse to lie because he values integrity.

On the other hand, external values come from outside of us. We tend to ignore external (superficial) values, especially when we think we can get away with it. For instance, think about the man who butts in the food line. This person has one standard for himself and another for everyone else. Obviously, he is asleep and living in the lower nature. Negative values will never lead to wholeness.

I encourage you to examine your values as you journey through this book. Values that hurt lead back to prison. Values of respect lead to a meaningful life.

CHANGE

One day a man saw a butterfly, shuddering on the sidewalk,
Locked in a seemingly hopeless struggle
To free itself from its now-useless cocoon.
Feeling pity, he took a pocketknife,
Carefully cut away the cocoon, and set the butterfly free.
To his dismay, it lay on the sidewalk,
Convulsed weakly for awhile, and died.
A biologist later told him,
"That was the worst thing you could have done!
A butterfly needs that struggle to develop the muscles to fly.
By robbing him of the struggle,
You made him too weak to live."

–Anonymous

Sue asked, "How does this story fit with values?"

"Our values might be wrong," I answered. "The man who tried to rescue the butterfly meant well, but lacked understanding." We must reevaluate our attempts to change others because of our values. Communication is the best way to deepen understanding.

Chapter 4

SPIRITUALITY

pirituality is a wonderful topic that we need to discuss for several reasons. First, anything that is not physical is spiritual. Spirituality separates humans from animals. As humans we have the ability to reflect and choose our responses to life. For example, I may not be able to do anything about sitting in jail, but I can certainly choose my attitude. Spirituality is our ability to rise above our lower self and choose a higher response.

Second, every time I teach a prison class I am reminded that the men are branded for life. No matter where you go, or what you do to redeem yourself, someone, somewhere, will point the finger at you and say, "He did time." You can live a life of integrity, but steal a loaf of bread, and you will be remembered as a thief. Spirituality offers hope and forgiveness.

After writing his daughter a letter, Isaac writes, "The soul searching of this assignment took a lot out of me and caused a lot of personal distress. The one thing that bothers me the most about myself is the terrible shame, guilt, and financial hardship that my incarceration caused my entire family."

Isaac needs to learn from the past, forgive himself, and move forward.

A third reason for discussing spirituality is my conviction that all people are spiritual. Of course, not everyone agrees with me.

Joby said, "I'm not a spiritual man. I don't believe in God. I can't stand religious people who profess to be righteous then rip people off."

I looked at Joby with feigned surprise, "I thought you told me that you were not spiritual? You seem spiritual to me."

He asked, "How so?"

I answered, "You just told me that you hate hypocrisy, but you value integrity and honesty. Aren't integrity and honesty spiritual qualities?"

Joby had never learned to see his integrity and honesty as spiritual. While religion offers us formalized doctrines about God, spirituality acknowledges the dignity of each person and the "oneness" of creation. Joby's decision to be honest and fair is a mark of spirituality.

DREAMS

"What does spirituality have to do with family?" you may wonder.

Everything! We already know that when someone sets a goal, he diligently strives to meet that objective. Every family needs a dream just as every person needs a goal. Dreams keep hope alive and offer direction and purpose.

Creation begins with a dream. Uncle Joe used to dream of traveling abroad. Aunt Gertie would shake her head and say, "It's never going to happen." He would just smile. Ironically, Uncle Joe and Aunt Gertie have now traveled to many of the places he once dreamed about. I encourage you to dream for yourself and your children. Our higher self hungers to journey beyond the edge. Columbus dreamed of discovering a new way to Asia. Betsy Ross dreamed her flag would become the symbol of the country she loved. Thomas Jefferson and Benjamin Franklin dreamed of a People's Republic. Rosa Parks and Martin Luther King, Jr. dreamed of equality for all. People who dare to dream are pioneers; they make a difference.

Without a dream we flounder in confusion. Remember the old saying, "When you don't know where you're going, any road will do"? Lack of hope and purpose lead to rebellion and despair. Rebellion results in injury and crime.

Dare to dream for yourself and your children, even from the isolation of prison. Men who dare to dream and climb toward the future, create a new life. Men who fail to dream, languish. Challenge your children to dream and create their future.

Hope and dreams are the fabric of spiritual life. Achieving our dreams leads to celebration and fulfillment.

DREAMS

I yearn for dreams just out of reach,
Bigger than one alone could fulfill.
Dreams so vast I don't know where to begin.
Sometimes, listening, I hear my future.
Enough to keep me hoping, wishing, knowing.
Nothing to disappoint or hinder.
Often I dream so much, I forget to listen to my heart,
Which beats to the endless rhythm, "You are a diamond."
Strange echoes of a voice I love.
It is hard to believe that place inside that cannot tell a lie.
As long as I remember to listen once in awhile,
My wishes will always come true.

–Angi Wolfgang

BOTTOM LINE

The bottom line–spirituality can be measured by how considerate we are of others, especially the weak. The spiritual man is conscious enough to protect the sacred and honorable in everyone. Mother Teresa said, "Unless life is lived for others, it is not worthwhile."

Spirituality begins with empathy or wearing our brother's shoes. Empathy is compassion, the bridge of relationship. When we have learned the golden rule of treating others the way we want to be treated, we are on the threshold of personal wholeness. Spiritual societies value justice, kindness, and empathy because they understand the equality of all people. "Do not hurt," bounces around the room from each corner of our heart. And at that moment, we are on the threshold of spiritual "oneness" with creation.

Albert raised his hand on the first day of class and asked with rage in his voice, "Are you going to talk about the conspiracy that put me here?" Albert is serving twenty years. For three months, Albert talked about the conspiracy, mostly by talking about "us"... incarcerated persons, and "them"...society and the conspirators.

US AND THEM

"Us" and "them" language divides people. If I do not like "them," I can assault them, enslave them, imprison them, or even destroy them.

On the other hand, when I begin to see the "oneness" of people, when I begin to realize that we are more alike than we are different, I can no longer isolate "them." I begin to understand that "we" all share the same hopes and dreams. Spiritual people realize that we are all connected to a beautiful drama that we do not fully understand.

Will our children learn "us versus them" language or "we" language? When fathers complain and use the language of blame, children learn to accuse. "We" language must be taught by parents who understand. Children who carry guns to school have not learned about "we" but have learned the language of hatred and fear—"us against them." Nothing destroys the human spirit quicker than abuse. Until understanding and empathy replace prejudice and abuse, hatred and hostility will flourish. Fences will go higher, more weapons will be sold, and society will be one step closer to civil war. Fathers, healthy families are vital to deal with a child's anger and rage; your children need you.

CHIEF SEATTLE

In 1852, the U.S. Government hoped to buy the tribal lands of native Indians. Chief Seattle wrote a marvelous letter in response to the government's inquiry. This letter is about the unity of everything:

> The President in Washington sends word that he wishes to buy our land. But how can you buy or sell the sky? The land? The idea is strange to us. If we do not own the freshness of the air and the sparkle of the water, how can you buy them?
>
> Every part of this earth is sacred to my people. Every shining pine needle, every sandy shore, every mist in the dark woods, every meadow, every humming insect. All are holy in the memory and experience of my people.

We know the sap which courses through the trees as we know the blood that courses through our veins. We are part of the earth and it is part of us. The perfumed flowers are our sisters. The bear, the deer, the great eagle, these are our brothers. The rocky crests, the juices in the meadow, the body heat of the pony, and man, all belong to the same family.

The shining water that moves in the streams and rivers is not just water, but the blood of our ancestors. If we sell you our land, you must remember that it is sacred. Each ghostly reflection in the clear waters of the lakes tells of events and memories in the life of my people. The water's murmur is the voice of my father's father.

The rivers are our brothers. They quench our thirst. They carry our canoes and feed our children. So you must give to the rivers the kindness you would give any brother.

If we sell you our land, remember that the air is precious to us, that the air shares its spirit with all the life it supports. The wind that gave our grandfather his first breath also receives his last sigh. The wind also gives our children the spirit of life. So if we sell you our land, you must keep it apart and sacred, as a place where man can go to taste the wind that is sweetened by the meadow flowers.

Will you teach your children what we have taught our children? That the earth is our mother? What befalls the earth befalls all the sons of the earth.

This we know: the earth does not belong to man, man belongs to the earth. All things are connected like the blood that unites us all. Man did not weave the web of life, he is merely a strand in it. Whatever he does to the web, he does to himself.

One thing we know: our god is also your god. The earth is precious to him and to harm the earth is to heap contempt on its creator.

Your destiny is a mystery to us. What will happen when the buffalo are all slaughtered? The wild horses tamed? What will happen when the secret corners of the forest are heavy with the scent of many men and the view of the ripe hills is blotted by talking wires? Where will the thicket be? Gone! Where will the eagle be? Gone! And what is it to say goodbye to the swift pony and the hunt? The end of living and the beginning of survival.

When the last Red Man has vanished with his wilderness, and his memory is only the shadow of a cloud moving across the prairie, will these shores and forests still be here? Will there be any of the spirit of my people left?

We love this earth as a newborn loves its mother's heartbeat. So, if we sell you our land, love it as we have loved it. Care for it as we have cared for it. Hold in your mind the memory of the land as it is when you receive it. Preserve the land for all children and love it, as God loves us all.

As we are part of the land, you too are part of the land. This earth is precious to us. It is also precious to you. One thing we know: there is only one God. No man, be he Red Man or White Man, can be apart. We are brothers after all.

Chief Seattle realizes the "oneness" of all things. His spiritual depth is timeless and rings true today. In the split second before reacting, the spiritual person catches himself to pause and to weigh the consequences of his behavior. Of course, unconscious men assume the pause is a sign of fear and weakness. But they are wrong; the pause of a wise man is not from personal fear but from fear of destroying a delicate unity. Chief Seattle teaches us that we destroy the chain of life by responding unconsciously.

Human beings now have the technological potential to destroy creation. As we have developed our consciousness, we have developed our power; we have enormous potential. Now, more than ever, we must assume consciousness for our world by living reflectively and empathetically. Seek awareness for yourself and your family. Bring healing and understanding. The greatest fear of a spiritual person is hurting the innocent. We will not inflict pain once we understand that we must also carry that pain and suffering.

THREE WORLDS
WORLD ONE

Let us imagine there are three worlds. The first world is the magical one that we first experience as a child, the world of confusion. Little Abby sees an elephant in the backyard because Abby does not know that elephants live in India, she just assumes India is her backyard. Magic and imagination rule this dream-like place. Eight-year-old Holly brags to sixteen-year-old Daniel, "I can run faster than you."

Mystical events defy explanation. Santa swooshes across the sky with his sleigh, stopping at every house, and sliding down every chimney with a sack full of gifts. His reindeer hang on the slippery roof and quietly wait while Santa eats a cookie and drinks his glass of milk. This is an innocent world of magic, enchantment, and awe.

When parents make this a world of warmth, safety, and laughter for their children, spontaneity and play are the natural consequence. Children play together and reach out to heal each other's hurt because there is no competition. This first world helps children develop imagination and intelligence.

WORLD TWO

The second world of enlightenment soon begins to bear down on the world of magic. The day when young Jonathan pretends to be Santa and gets stuck in the chimney, science gets her foot in the door. Enlightenment is the awakening of the mind to discovery and difference. In world two, everything has its place, and everything is studied. We divide life into categories: either we are male or female, sad or happy, gay or straight, winner or loser, rich or poor, Republican or Democrat. In this world we study cause and effect, borders and boundaries, distinguishing between subject and object. We dissect the macro to study the micro. Scientific method helps us define and isolate the particulars. This is the world of programs and education; academic credentials go to those who learn the answers. In the scientific world, we strive to master the mystery. Categories and classifications become substitutes for large amounts of scientific data. We quickly learn that this world is polarized and competitive. It is the Titanic against the iceberg and cancer against life. We learn to battle and strive for superiority: "survival of the fittest." Our culture places a high priority on mastery of this second world; high achievers are rewarded with power and possessions.

PARADOX

The second world falters when we are confronted with suffering and paradox, which is the threshold of the third world. The paradox is our ability to simultaneously see both sides of the same coin: the sunrise is the sunset; sorrow is the fountain of joy. Third world citizens unite the objective and subjective. We are no longer comfortable with answers but look for the ever present questions that are hidden in shadows and symbolism. At this point, language fails us because it is both too literal and not literal enough. Language becomes illusive; words are symbols with multiple interpretations. Every sentence is pregnant with experience, fear, hope, and belief.

WORLD THREE

Paradox opens into the mysterious third world of "oneness." We may not be conscious of the change, but one day we wake up never to see life the same again. Interdependence and wholeness are now more apparent than independence or dependence. Duality is replaced by integration, polarity by community. We move beyond distinctions of light and dark, us and them, good and evil, black and white, pleasure and pain. Music is enhanced by the space and time between the notes; art is a reflection of the unpainted canvas. We have now discovered it is the negative space that makes the positive image; the background enhances the foreground. Both dark and light are vital to life. While we must experience life outwardly to understand the balance, we must experience life inwardly to understand the "oneness." Beauty and balance erupt from this mysterious wholeness. Although wholeness is uncomfortable because it is neither black nor white, yin nor yang, it is complete. This third world is filled only with beauty, only with balance, only with suffering, only with music, only with silence, only with God. Categories are useless; there is only one picture. Chief Seattle is right, "We are part of the earth and it is part of us."

The language of this mysterious world is symbolic and whole. Roles are more essential than rules. Citizens of the third world have a way of standing everything on its head. We respect even the mud for its gift to life. We treat one another with dignity because it is within us. Whatever we do to another eventually returns to us. Creation is a complete circle; there is an energetic connection and synchronicity of all. If we break the chain, we reap the consequences. Fear and love are the only emotions, and one without the other is meaningless.

In this world of oneness, the animate and inanimate mirror one another. The animate world creates time and awareness. The inanimate world brings value and stability. One cannot exist without the other; together we create our existence.

MIRRORS...

Laughter is the mirror of wisdom
The self is the mirror of God
Your smile mirrors my acceptance
Integrity mirrors spirituality
Male mirrors female
Rocks mirror eternity
Love mirrors esteem
Empathy mirrors connection
Stories mirror meaning
Time mirrors value
Anger mirrors pain
Fear mirrors love
Life mirrors hope
You mirror me

–Wolfgang

At this point, we understand that even a lie springs from the truth. Scientific analysis is no longer enough; we hunger to understand the completeness, which never seems to get smaller—just simpler and more complex. Every answer becomes a question. This is why third world citizens will often respond to a question with, "It depends." We are not trying to be illusive but reflective because truth and understanding slowly unfold. Truth and beauty are the synchronous total of all reality, not just my perception.

This third world can only be learned through experience. Suffering, passion, pleasure, beauty, fear, anguish, and love are all avenues that lead us here. We must relinquish security and control to enter this sacred realm where we experience collective awareness: Self. Only the courageous, vulnerable, and awe-seeking can walk here. In this third world, every smile is returned, every dollar is earned, and every being is offered an opportunity to contribute.

Mirrors and guides to the third world surround us, but we will not see them until we open our hearts; then we wonder how we missed them.

APPLE

Take an apple. The first world enjoys the fruit because of an unconscious hunger. The second world slices the apple, analyzes the ingredients, and observes the apple in its natural environment. Knowledge about the apple is more important than the apple. The third world becomes an apple, consciously appreciating the feel, the aroma, the taste and even the worm. The pleasure of biting an apple is best learned by experience.

Spirituality begins in the world of magic with the relationship between child and parent. In the beginning, the child wakes up convinced that he is invincible; he knows all the answers to life. This naïve but dogmatic world soon collapses under suffering and pain, which lead to introspection and reflection. Out of this reflection, our unconscious seeks answers, and truth begins to unfold.

Pain is deeper than all thought;
Laughter is higher than all pain.

–Elbert Hubbart

Understanding gradually leads to acceptance and appreciation, which begin the third world of mystery and beauty. In this mysterious world, spirituality is the collective experience of all people. Demello writes, "If you have one watch, you know the time. If you have two watches, you're never sure." Living in the third world is never certain but enchanting.

Third world men are equalizers. They speak for the unconscious and powerless because they create balance and fairness. Just as Chief Seattle speaks "we" language for "...the great eagle... the wild horses...the ripe hills...the shining water," equalizers stand between the powerful and their prey. They frustrate the greedy and powerful by leveling the field for the innocent and poor. Equality, fairness, and respect govern their desire for pleasure, power, and security.

The highest honors of history belong to men and women who embraced the equalizer spirit. These noble people built dreams and nations that have benefited humankind. At some basic level, we acknowledge the virtue and wholeness of such courage.

The spiritual journey must begin inside, in solitude. Sit silently in the darkness. Then reach into the muddle for your fear. Listen to your pain, listen to your weakness, and listen to your anxiety. What is fear saying? Understanding begins with inner awakening.

> *... come into this Darkness which is beyond light, and, without seeing and without knowing, see and know that which is above vision and knowledge.*
>
> *—Dionysius*

Until we know our fear, we cannot know our hope. Until we know our suffering, we cannot know our joy. Until we know our turmoil, we cannot know our peace. Until we parent ourselves, we cannot parent our children. We cannot heal others until we understand healing. We cannot love others until we experience love. We cannot teach others until we have become conscious. We cannot teach justice until we understand balance. The darkness is your friend. Invite the blackness to swallow you and teach you. Surprisingly, you will learn about the light.

The journey of life is between fear and desire. Until you accept your fear, you will be violent. Until you accept your desire, you will be driven. Until you accept your darkness, you will be lost. Make peace in the darkness.

Ryan said, "Fear is your friend, it shows you the way."

Aha! That is the sound of the wind! We are imprisoned with unconscious chains until we name our fear; then, we are free to move beyond.

THE MAN IN THE GLASS

When you get what you want in your struggle for self
And the world makes you king for a day,
Just go to a mirror and look at yourself,
And see what that man has to say.

For it isn't your father or mother or wife
Whose judgment upon you must pass;
The fellow whose verdict counts most in your life
Is the one staring back from the glass.

Some people might think you're a straight-shootin' chum
And call you a wonderful guy.
But the man in the glass says you're only a bum
If you can't look him straight in the eye.

He's the fellow to please, never mind all the rest,
For he's with you clear to the end,
And you've passed your most dangerous test
If the guy in the glass is your friend.

You may fool the whole world down the pathway of years
And get pats on the back as you pass.
But your final reward will be heartache and tears
If you've cheated the man in the glass.

–*Author unknown*

Gentlemen, when we try to escape the deeds of our past, we fall into a pattern of pretense and denial. Pretense and denial drain as much energy as confession and honesty. Refuse to be chained by your self-pity and fear of self-improvement. Accept yourself, the total package, and grow. Above all others, you know that our society must be built on integrity and forgiveness. Become a friend, the kind of friend you want in your suffering. Our families and communities suffer without men willing to answer the call to fatherhood.

INMATES, FROM NOW ON ...

From now on, you understand freedom
From now on, you understand courage
From now on, you understand strength
From now on, you understand love
From now on, you understand suffering
From now on, you understand racism
From now on, you understand kindness
From now on, you understand hope
From now on, what will you choose?

–Wolfgang

Chapter 5

TRAPS

ANGER

Cindy answers the phone with a sob, "Hello."

"What's the matter, Babe?" Randy asks.

"Oh, the baby just spilled her milk on the computer, and Len called to say the car needs a transmission. It could cost 1,500 dollars. I don't see how we're going to get through this."

Randy feels the knot starting in his stomach. He says, "Cindy, how could you let the baby near the computer? Can't you keep Beth at the table when she's eating?"

Randy and Cindy begin arguing, and Randy wonders why he bothered to call. Why can't Cindy understand? Jail is cold! Randy wants a little warmth and romance. He wants to know that he is missed and loved. Instead, Cindy begins to complain about her problems and the bills. Randy feels the acid in his belly and turns on Cindy for not controlling little Beth. His expectation of a warm conversation is quickly dying.

"I can't take this anymore," he said, "doesn't she understand? I've got enough to deal with in jail. I'm gonna cut her loose, I don't need this aggravation."

If Randy stops calling Cindy, Beth will lose contact with her father. How will she understand Dad's neglect? She will think that Dad does not care about her.

"Traps" destroy family life and intimacy. Abuse, aggression, anger, criticism, blame, shame, withdrawal, hatred, self-pity, prejudice, depression, and fear are a few of these traps. Instead of fostering intimacy and growth, traps destroy our relationships and diminish personal wholeness.

Let us begin with anger. Anger is a broad emotion that includes excitement, fear, hurt, disappointment, and blame.

Believe it or not, anger may be healthy. Fear is a built-in alarm that triggers our anger and alerts us to danger. I want my children to get angry about destruction, abuse, and prejudice. This anger provides information that helps us respond appropriately.

UNRESOLVED ANGER

But there is a type of anger responsible for untold pain and suffering: unresolved anger. Unresolved anger is the dark, repressed anger that destroys our spirit. We are victimized, and although we struggle to understand why anyone would abuse us, the answer eludes us. Out of this hurt and suffering come depression, self-pity, and worthlessness. The longer we carry this baggage, the more intense our anger becomes. Before long, the venom of resentment, bitterness, and rage have taken root. Unchecked, unresolved anger explodes in aggression, hate, and violence. The crime and violence infecting our communities started as anger and the violation of someone's dignity.

A wounded spirit cannot rest,
He plans and schemes to settle the debt.
The anger mounts, the rage intent,
A tortured soul, hell bound sent.

–Wolfgang

Unresolved anger can only be released by returning to the source of the suffering and pain. I encourage my students to write letters of confession to those who have injured their trust. These are not letters of accusation and blame but letters of personal hurt and anguish (Two examples may be found in the opening chapter on trust). By confessing the pain and injury, we break the powerful cycle of this progressive and destructive anger.

Randy wants Cindy's affection. But instead of talking to Cindy about his need, he blames her. How is she the cause of his frustration? Blaming Cindy will leave her with unresolved anger and certainly not help Randy get the affection that he wants. Blame and criticism destroy relationships.

Ronald wrote to his son who refused to write back. It was hard for Ronald to understand Ty's silence. But silence and withdrawal is a natural reaction to deep hurt. Now Ronald expects to sweep into Ty's life and overcome years of neglect with a letter. Although Ty loves his father, he is bitter and refuses to break the painful silence. After all, Dad injured Ty with silent neglect. Ronald may win Ty's trust if he is willing to hear his son's pain and anger. Dad must persistently reach out to his son. Listening to the anguish of our children and rebuilding trust are the only hope for mending relationships.

> ***Anger would inflict punishment on another, meanwhile, it tortures itself.***
>
> ***–Publilius Syrus***

Most incarcerated men live with the fear that someone is "hitting on" their spouse. Instead of building intimacy through genuine concern and care, these men repeatedly accuse their women of promiscuous behavior. What is wrong with this picture? Joe Player is incarcerated, but he is trying to police his wife.

JUAN

Juan married his high school sweetheart. One afternoon he came home early to find his wife in bed with his friend. The relationship ended in a nasty divorce; thank God there were no children.

In time, Juan meets Betty and they fall in love. They live together for eight years and have three children before Juan is incarcerated. Now Juan is going bonkers. He calls Betty every day, sometimes twice a day, to check up on her, "Where have you been? What have you been doing? Where were you last night?"

Juan asks his brother to tail Betty, and one night he happens to see her car at the Brass Frog Tavern. Juan goes ballistic. He cannot sleep, he threatens to break her legs and take the children.

Betty changes her phone number and threatens to move if Juan does not stop stalking her—from jail.

The first time I meet Juan, he looks haggard and unkempt. Of course, he expects me to fix his marriage. Maybe I'll end up with the broken legs?

I challenge Juan to back off and give his wife distance. Juan cannot see it because he is blinded with fear and self-pity. Juan is unconsciously blaming Betty for the pain caused by his first wife. When will Juan begin to take responsibility for his own life instead of blaming Betty? For nearly three months we talk about Juan's demon of fear, and slowly he takes some responsibility for the failed relationship. Eventually he confesses, "I treated my wife like a dog on a chain."

Juan begins to write to his children and focus his love on them. In time, he writes to Betty and tells her the painful secret of his first marriage. Betty is struggling financially, so Juan agrees to sell a plot of land to support his children, no strings attached. Ever so slowly, Juan and Betty begin to talk. For three months, Juan listens to Betty's unresolved anger, pain, and bitterness. Slowly the relationship begins to heal. The week before Juan's release, he told me with a huge smile that Betty had agreed to meet him for dinner.

Do not allow the demon of fear to drive away your love. The secret of Juan's relationship to Betty is respect. Respect is vital to every relationship. When respect ends, the relationship dies. We must learn to trust our wives, listen to their struggles, and support them. They will return our love and tenderness.

This brings us to a game that men know very well, walking out and slamming the door. "If you don't see it my way, baby, I'm outta here." This is the most devastating way to hurt those who love us. Attacking the relationship is hitting below the belt. Tell her what you want instead of trying to control the relationship through threats, cruelty, and domination.

FAMILY

The greatest misnomer about incarceration, bar none, is that incarceration is most difficult for the prisoner. While I do not want to minimize the loss of freedom and life in a 5 x 7 steel and block cage, innocent families, spouses, and children pay an enormous price for incarceration. For example, if there is a lot of publicity about the event, children are shunned and ridiculed. When Cheyenne's father cannot attend her high school graduation, tongues wag about his crime.

The pressure of incarceration on a marriage is unfathomable. Often, families must move to another location; children change schools and find new friends. Spouses assume responsibility for the family, legal matters, and finances. Loneliness, fear, betrayal, loss, frustration, and isolation tear at the spouse and children. Children who have been abandoned by their father want to know if he will care about them when he is released.

WEEKENDS

On the weekend, your lady gets her hair done, arranges for childcare, gases the car, locks the house, and then drives the stressful interstate toward prison. She feels alone on a strange road, the weather threatening. And while she is happy to see you, it is not easy to walk into a place that is holding her husband captive.

She patiently waits to be processed into the visiting room only to have you say, "What took you so long?" During the visit, you lay on her your frustration and the work you expect her to finish during the week. After the visit and the heartbreaking goodbye, she silently heads for home under the cover of darkness. She often wonders, "Will he care about me once he is released?" Depression hovers nearby, but she must pick up the children and become a mother again.

Gentlemen, would you visit her the way she visits you?

SHE'S ALWAYS BEEN THAT WAY

She knows my needs before I do; she's always been that way.
She walks before me just to clear all my fears away.
She hears my faintest whisper and sees my smallest tear,
She tells me there's a reason as to why they put me here.

She knows my faults and failings, the times that I complain,
My trials and tribulations, the plans that we have made.

She says it doesn't matter, and it all will pass away,
That I only need to trust her, so her love can come to stay.

So I take the bits and pieces of this life I've come to know,
And I tell her that I love her as I did so long ago.
I feel my burden lifted, and I know that come what may,
Her love for me is endless, 'cause she's always been that way.

–Juan

RELEASING ANGER

There are two ways to release anger. The wrong way is through abuse and uncontrolled rage. Unresolved anger goes deep into the gut and gnaws at us with ulcers, headaches, back pain, and depression. The angry person may pretend to be cool, but inside he feels cold. The coldness reminds me of rubbing alcohol, cool to the touch but just waiting for a spark. Sometimes something trivial, like a shove on the basketball court, ignites the explosion, and "Jake" gets his teeth knocked out.

I have met too many wives who are victims of physical abuse. Abusers have a problem that will never be solved by beating a loved one. Abusive patterns destroy our families and continue to the grandchildren. If you beat your wife and children, for God's sake, get therapy.

SHAWN

Shawn used to come to class and "chill." He rarely talked, and I silently prayed for some way to connect with him before the end of the program. One day I just decided to take the risk and jump.

"Shawn, I don't really know you. I know you are "short" (i.e., Shawn is counting the months, instead of years, until his release). My gut tells me that you are being pulled in two directions. On one hand, it seems you're being pulled to return to your son and be a father. I believe that is why you joined this class. If you have the courage to return to your family, I think you will be happy. On the other hand, it seems you are being pulled back to the street because of the anger inside of you. You have talent buried under deep anger. If you return to the street, I'm afraid your rage will cause you to die violently or go to jail for a long time."

Shawn just looked at me, his expression never changing. I began to fear that maybe I had made a mistake. But doggoned, somehow I hoped to reach this young father.

"Mr. Wolfgang, I haven't said much in this class, but I've been listening and taking it in. You're right. I started taking this class because I'm having trouble with my son's mother. I hoped this class would help me learn how to be a better father. But I am so angry with my ex that I can't sleep at night. All I think about is how to make her feel the pain that she's causing me. Right now I can't get to her, but the dead rise. If she won't let me talk to my son and won't let me see him when I go home, I don't know what I'll do. I'm just gonna say, that will not happen, I will be with my son."

The class sat quietly. We could feel Shawn's hurt through the tension in his voice. I felt apprehensive that someone would say the wrong thing. Michael broke the silence.

"Shawn, this is my third bit. I've spent most of my life in prison. You remind me of me. The first time I went down, I wasted time. Then I was out for a year and back in. Now I got twenty years. I'm not a young man like you; I wish I could do it over again. I bet your baby's mother is involved with another man, and now that you're short, she's nervous about you coming home. Know what I mean? I know that you're angry with your ex, and it's not right the way she's treating you by trying to cut you out of your son's life. But if you go after her and her man, you're gonna be right back here with me. You got to get on with your life because your son needs you."

Michael had done it; he stepped up to the plate and belted out a homer. Shawn listened intently because Michael had paid dearly for his mistakes.

Shawn signed up for the Parenting II classes and began talking about his son and ex-wife. Slowly, we watched the cold, hard Shawn melt and a new, smiling, energetic young man take his place. Shawn still had a difficult time dealing with his ex, but he began to make progress when he realized that he needed to make peace with her and her boyfriend if he hoped for a good relationship with his son.

RISING UP...

It was a cold December day. We were crowded into the small classroom, the one with art hanging on the walls because it doubles as an art room. The men sat in their coats because of the chill blowing through the block walls. How could I have known that this was the day I would see Shawn rise from the dead?

"This week I've been thinking about the way I treated my ex-wife and son," he said. "Up to now, I have been angry at my ex for cutting me out of my son's life. But when I think back to my time on the street, I didn't do her right. Some nights I never went home. And I never helped her take care of the baby. She used to beg me to get off the street; I thought I was being a good father and husband by paying the bills and giving her extra money. Sometimes she would just throw the money at me. Really, I can't say I blame my wife for her attitude and not wanting me to be around her or my son."

I could feel the peace coming into my heart. You see, when someone discovers empathy, he is no longer blind. Shawn's relationship with his ex and son would be different from now on.

A BETTER WAY

A better way to release anger is to follow the pattern of Shawn. When Shawn began to take responsibility for his behavior, he began to heal. Not only did Shawn's attitude toward his wife change, but his whole attitude toward life changed. His frown was replaced with a smile, his gloominess with spontaneity, and his silence with emotion.

End the cold, hard silence by talking about your anger. Write letters that confess your hurt and pain to those who offended you. Remember, the letter is not about blame; instead, it is a record of your suffering. Keep a journal or talk to someone strong enough to hear your anguish. This is much better than being enslaved by rage and revenge. Venting anger in the presence of acceptance and respect will allow you to release the burden and grow instead of wasting priceless energy on pretense. It is important to share anger frequently because incarceration creates anger and frustration.

Therapists talk about differentiation. This is the ability to separate our emotion from our behavior. A child who is disappointed may throw a temper tantrum, getting down on the floor kicking and screaming. The child's anger controls his behavior. Mature adults, like Juan and Shawn, learn to differentiate (separate) their emotions from their behavior. In other words, responsible adults control the lower self (impulses) with the higher self (mind).

Anger and aggression are different. Anger is an important and valid emotion. Aggression is injuring another person. While I accept my child's anger, I disapprove of her aggression and hostility. Adults select healthy outlets for anger and control their aggression.

PREJUDICE

At the center of human suffering is the evil of ignorance and prejudice. Mel was a victim of racism and has the scars to prove it. If anyone disagrees with Mel, he throws the prejudice card...sometimes under his breath. Of course, Mel has the right to question prejudice and injustice; he has suffered deeply. But Mel has been hiding behind his hatred for so long that he cannot move beyond it. He told me, "Whenever I am offended, I conjure up all the anger and hate from my past." To Mel's credit, he has become aware of his anger and is working toward renewal. Mel must begin to focus outwardly on change instead of inwardly on rage.

Prejudice is war; in ignorance, it destroys the human spirit.

DEPRESSION

Depression is anger turned inwardly against the self, as opposed to aggression, which is anger turned outwardly toward others. Depression, or the lack of hope, saps our energy and is often accompanied by feelings of shame, silence, and contempt for self. When we are depressed, little things irritate us even as we emotionally withdraw. Healing begins with acceptance and confession. Until the self-hatred is shared, it eats at us like cancer. We must re-create acceptance and hope for ourselves instead of living in isolation and self-pity. Today, there are wonderful therapies for depression.

Approximately two million children have incarcerated fathers. Father neglect causes depression (hopelessness), apathy (not caring), and rebellion (anger) among children. The cost of rehabilitating these children will balloon in the coming century. This is an epidemic we cannot afford and a tragedy that children do not deserve.

STRESS

Long days at work, financial pressures, family concerns, and unresolved conflict create stress. In turn, we pass this stress to our children. Our hardened tones and sharp responses make children feel unworthy and unimportant. Stress will destroy our relationships if it leads to criticism and blame.

ABUSE

Another trap that we need to discuss is abuse. Approximately twenty-five percent (25%) of girls and fourteen percent (14%) of boys experience abuse. Abuse damages our emotions. Like wounded animals, we crawl away to hide in fear or retaliate with rage.

Abuse is a misuse of power. It begins with resentment and ends with the violation of an innocent victim, often a child or spouse. Abusers are former victims of abuse who harbor unresolved anger and bitterness. In turn, they pass their broken spirit onto others.

Sexual abuse is more than the desire for sexual gratification; it is about the misuse of power and aggression. Victims of sexual abuse rarely recover and the abuse adversely affects their other relationships. Sexual abuse violates intimacy.

Verbal abuse is cutting another person with cruel words. I remember walking through the mall and hearing a mother yell at her son, "Come here, Shithead." How does this child feel about himself? How will he learn to parent his children?

Please do not slam your child with cruel words. Stupid, fat, dumb, lazy, ugly, retard, moron, and bonehead are words that destroy a child's spirit and beauty. No one enjoys being humiliated. Attempts to control a child's behavior through humiliation and shame never work but end in rebellion and depression. Learn to talk with your child. Learn to be angry without being cruel.

Emotional abuse humiliates the child by withholding love and tenderness for selfish reasons. Never tell your child, "I won't love you anymore," or "I'm going to give you away." There are better ways to discipline than to threaten neglect. Every child deserves unconditional love. However, parents will find it difficult to love unconditionally if they have never received it themselves.

Neglect is failure to meet the basic needs of children. Dad is on the street taking care of his "player" addiction while Mom is cuddling with Jack Daniels. If we think about it, neglect is severe abuse because it does not teach the skills necessary for social interaction.

Physical abuse violates another person and their dignity. This includes slapping them on the face, neglect, beatings, torture, and injury. Physical abuse is never about discipline, but about unresolved anger and rage in the parent. I beg you, seek help if you are physically abusing your child; you deserve healing.

ABUSE TEACHES CHILDREN TO:

SHUT UP! –Do not talk about anything important.
SHUT OUT! –Do not feel the hurt and pain.
SHUT DOWN! –Do not care about anyone but self.

Abused children frequently resort to abnormal behavior such as lying, stealing, and aggression because of the unresolved hurt and pain. These children need affection, security, and understanding. Hostility and ridicule further shatter their self-esteem; it is important to respond to them in a firm but gentle manner.

Young children may confuse sadness and anger because they do not know how to be sad. If a child responds to you with anger, hear the child's frustration. Anger makes us defensive, but we must allow anger if we ever hope to achieve intimacy. I tell my children, "You have a right to be angry; I will not allow you to be cruel." Encouragement, affection, trust, and time are the best way for parents to learn about unresolved hurt and abuse.

CYCLE OF ABUSE:

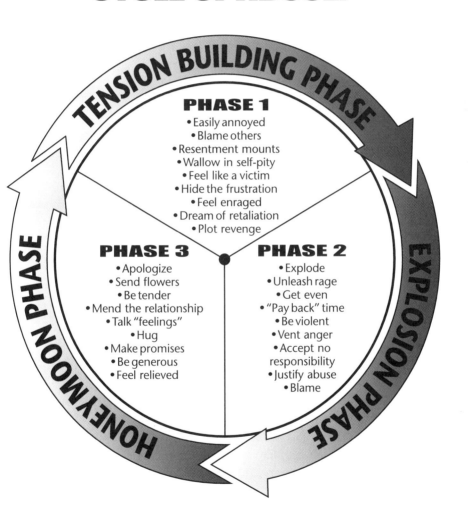

TENSION BUILDING PHASE

EXPLOSION PHASE

HONEYMOON PHASE

PHASE 1
- Easily annoyed
- Blame others
- Resentment mounts
- Wallow in self-pity
- Feel like a victim
- Hide the frustration
- Feel enraged
- Dream of retaliation
- Plot revenge

PHASE 3
- Apologize
- Send flowers
- Be tender
- Mend the relationship
- Talk "feelings"
- Hug
- Make promises
- Be generous
- Feel relieved

PHASE 2
- Explode
- Unleash rage
- Get even
- "Pay back" time
- Be violent
- Vent anger
- Accept no responsibility
- Justify abuse
- Blame

THE THOUSAND WORDS

Better than a thousand useless words
Is one word which brings peace.
Better than a thousand useless verses
Is one line which brings joy.
Better than a thousand useless poems
Is one poem which brings love.

'...He abused me, he struck me,
he overcame me, he robbed me,'
in those who harbor such thoughts
hatred will never cease.
'He abused me, he struck me,
he overcame me, he robbed me,'
in those who do not harbor such thoughts
hatred will cease.

–The Dhammaphada

SHAME AND GUILT

Shame and guilt accompany each other, but they are not the same. Guilt comes from knowing that I have done wrong, from breaking a moral code. Guilt is a consequence of my behavior. Shame occurs when I fall short of others' expectations. For example, "Why can't you be like your sister?" Or, "Dan is a better basketball player than you!" Comparisons bring shame.

Shame affects the self. I felt guilty when I kicked Ally, our cat, into the bush; I felt ashamed because my daughter Andi saw me.

Shame and guilt are like different sides of the same coin. Forgiveness and restitution help amend guilt. But like a scar, shame wounds our spirit for eternity.

However broken down is the spirit's shrine,
The spirit is there all the same.

–Nigerian Proverb

Hispanic students have taught me that shame separates us from the animals. Like medicine, a dose of shame teaches us humility and empathy. Conversely, too much shame and guilt breed rebellion, despair, and illness.

Shame comes from the deep belief that I do not belong —anywhere. It is rooted deeply in the spirit and destroys our self-worth, leading to self-pity. In turn, when our children fail at something, we are embarrassed because we believe their failure reflects on us. Therefore, we make a big deal out of their failure and shame them. Shame will damage relationships until it is confessed and healed.

FAMILY SHAME

Families cause shame. Incarcerated men have taught me that illegal activity often benefits the family, yet when the person is incarcerated, he feels shunned. The family gladly accepted the economic benefits of crime but turns away when the offender is caught. This may result in a sense of shame so strong that the person denies the pain. Instead, he blames forces outside of himself for the internal rage. As he learns to accept responsibility for his behavior, he is on the way to healing.

FATHER SHAME

The father role has changed significantly over the past few decades. Not a hundred years ago, fathers were expected to provide shelter, safety, and sustenance for their family. Men grew up with culturally defined roles that were clear and rarely questioned. Men worked in the fields, factories, and forges while women attended to the various matters of home life. The last few decades have drastically changed fathering roles, and we have lost our way. While most fathers still feel the need to provide for their families, many feel like failures in our highly competitive society. For instance, if I cannot afford a modest standard of living for my family or my marriage is "on the rocks," I may feel crushed by inadequacy and failure. To escape this burden, I channel my energy into sports, work, aggression, promiscuity, or even criminal activity. These activities tend to reinforce the masculine image.

There have been dark moments when I am absolutely positive that my family would be better off without me. Face it, fatherhood is not an easy responsibility; many men find being single an attractive alternative to family life. Once, during one of these dark moments, my daughter said to me, "Dad, I love it when our family is together, and you tease us." At that moment, my daughter helped me understand that failure in my eyes may not be failure to her. Our families can help us understand our role as husband and father when we feel lost. We must learn to trust them and not fear the darkness.

CHILD SHAME

Make no mistake, incarcerated fathers pass shame on to their children. In turn, this shame affects a child's behavior. When fathers accept responsibility for their shame and the shame of their children, they help their children heal. I challenge you, write to each member of your family, and ask how your incarceration embarrasses him. Please do not allow your children to deceive you because you are too fragile to hear the truth. Dialogue (communication) breaks the cycle of shame.

Cornell showed me the letter his teenager wrote. The son denied his incarcerated father ever caused him shame. How about the times Junior had to write a report for school and make up stories about his absent dad? Maybe Junior is afraid to tell his father how he really feels because his honest confession might hurt Dad.

PERSONAL SHAME

Shame also stems from personal characteristics that we believe are unacceptable and lacking. Size, age, looks, illness, work, neighborhood, social status, failure, and even success can cause shame. We live in a critical society; children know what style of shoe they must wear to avoid ridicule. My nephew squeezed his size seven feet into popular basketball shoes that were size five because according to Cory, "Aren't these awesome?" Shame is reinforced every time we are reminded, "You just don't measure up."

I recently overheard a mother yelling at her daughter, "I'm not buying you nothing 'cause you're no good. I'm buying this for Emily, but not for you because you're bad." When the child started to cry and refused to move from her spot on the floor, Mom went out the front door threatening, "I'm leaving you here; I don't care about you anymore." How can we expect our child to learn wholeness when we assault her fragile spirit?

ELLEN

"I think everyone has some shame...sometimes we don't even realize what it is. I also think we are shamed about our greatest pain. The pain makes us sensitive and caring and empathetic. When I was nine, I remember going to Camp Rainwater. We were swimming and I walked over to a boy I recognized from school. I said, 'Hi, Jeremy, do you remember me? I used to be in your class at school.' He looked at me and said, 'I don't remember fat people's names.' I felt very shameful. I didn't know what to say or do. I was so embarrassed and humiliated. It took a lot of courage for me to say anything to him to begin with...and then, a response like that...I wanted to cry and cry. But people were all around, so I couldn't cry. I think I feel that being overweight is my fault, and if I just had more discipline, or strength, or something, I would be thin. So I feel guilty about it, like I'm not a strong enough person to make myself skinny. And so sometimes when I think about it, I feel worthless and not lovable. I always question David and ask him if he loves me because I can't believe he would love someone like me. But I guess everyone feels that way about something; everyone has something in his or her life they are shamed about. Like you said, they have been called ugly or fat or stupid or worthless, and just like that one time sticks in my mind...that's all it takes...just one time. I can't even imagine people who have been abused all their lives."

TEDDY

Nine-year-old Teddy looked around before he reached into the cookie jar. Something inside made him do it although this game was not about cookies anymore. Every time Mom caught Teddy, she smacked his fingers. Later he would try again. How could Teddy know that if his mother did not catch him, he would someday graduate to larger games? Teddy is already learning the cycle of shame and disobedience.

Why does Teddy keep reaching into the cookie jar? He knows he might get caught. Teddy refuses to give up because shame makes him feel worthless and rejected. Naturally, he resents this negative image and works diligently to change it. Teddy's behavior is a consequence of shame, and his problem is deeper than his craze with the cookie jar. Teddy is hungry for affection and affirmation; he needs to see his own beauty.

Let us switch to the courtroom. Ted, now twenty-two years old, stands before Judge Riley who wants "Theodore" to feel the shame of his crime. Ted knows the game; he played it with his mother. The Judge points at Ted, who pretends to feel the humiliation, hoping it will lighten his sentence. But Ted has learned to bend his knees and not his heart. He is still starved for affection and desperate to find his beauty.

Ted is sentenced to 115 months. He turns numbly toward his mother and wife and son, who all cry as he is cuffed and led away. Ted does not realize that his numbness will eventually turn to bitterness and rage, leading him toward revenge. Teddy Jr. is too young to know that he will be thirteen years old (13) before his father is released—the first time. By then Teddy Jr. will have the same hunger for affection and beauty as his father.

Shame is a powerful motivator. Teddy Jr. stole a Bulls jacket because it is "awesome." The bully shames his victim, but the victim gets even with a handgun. As our society becomes more critical and intolerant, crime increases.

HEALING SHAME

The secret of healing shame is tolerance and acceptance of the inner self. We must learn to give ourselves the same respect we give others. Become a child; enjoy life for the first time instead of withdrawing in criticism and self-pity. Like suffering, deep shame connects to the soul and becomes a part of our identity. How can we pull away from something that defines us? Unfortunately, shame cannot be tossed away like garbage. Instead, it must be reintegrated into our personality as a source of understanding and compassion. Revisit your shame and forgive yourself. Embrace shame and transform it into character and empathy, thereby creating the potential for intimacy. Shame can be a fountain of beauty because it may be turned into friendship.

Shame asks about the meaning of life and deepens us spiritually. Personal awareness is expanded, and we develop a new appreciation for ALL of life's experiences. Embrace your shame. A wise proverb says, "The teacher appears when the student is ready." In other words, "The curse is the gift."

Wounds of shame, guilt, hurt, and pain can fester and cause havoc. Or, the wounds can heal and bring understanding. Understanding heals! Only the healed can heal others.

Fathers, before it is too late, talk to Teddy. Communication counteracts shame because it shows value. Hold Teddy tenderly, even on the phone, through acceptance and warmth. Laugh together, tease, and cherish the gift of your child. Fathering your child will help you confront your own shame.

AN INSTRUMENT OF PEACE

Lord, make me an instrument of your peace,
Where there is hatred, let me sow love;
Where there is injury, pardon;
Where there is doubt, faith;
Where there is despair, hope;
Where there is darkness, light;
Where there is sadness, joy.
O Divine master,
Grant that I may not so much seek
To be consoled as to console,
To be understood as to understand
To be loved as to love;

For it is in giving that we receive,
It is in pardoning that we are pardoned,
And it is in dying that we are born to eternal life.

–Saint Francis of Assisi

FEAR

Fear is a primary emotion. Fear...and love are the roots of all suffering...and joy. We love because we fear: "I love the warmth because I fear the cold." On the other hand, we fear because we love: "I fear losing you because I love you." Fear and love are primary emotions.

Fear creates a "fight or flight" response. It drives us to control or destroy those who threaten us. Most of us live with unconscious fear that spills over into arrogance, deceit, betrayal, perfectionism, abuse, stress, disease, and even war.

Fear may be rational or irrational. Rational fear is reasonable and understandable. Irrational fear is much more common, and of course, more bizarre. There are times when irrational fear consumes an entire community.

Many of our streets and schools are concrete jungles of fear because of the violence. But violence does not begin on the street; violence begins with fear. Heartfelt fear creates the desperate grab for security and power that ends in brutality. And fear is not limited to the "neighborhood." Corporate America has been lining the pockets of investors, even as low and middle class America struggle with record amounts of debt. Ultimately, this strategy fails to build enduring communities of peace. When greed brings suffering to our neighbor, fear, deceit, and violence are not far behind.

Ryan said, "Fear is your friend, it shows you the way." Not all fear is negative; fear shows us our weakness and inspires us to develop new potential. Men, it is time for us to confront the fear that is controlling our lives, our children, and our community. How can we idly stand by as our children are victimized by fear? Our children cannot talk until we talk. We must begin to model healing roles; together we can work our way through this epidemic of violence; together we can find solidarity. Life is a team effort; we must rededicate ourselves to unity and balance, or we all lose. Until unity becomes important, the day of death will thrive.

WHY DO I CRY?

Why do I cry, everybody asks me.
People tell me to be strong or to have courage.
How, I ask, can I be strong when inside
I am dying and I hurt so much?

It's hard to live away from my children.
Tears of sadness fill my eyes,
And through my tears I alleviate the pain.
My tears reflect the love I feel for them.

My friend, that's why I cry, so don't say
That I am afraid or that I am a coward.
The pain I bear inside of me is so great
That I carry it with me wherever I go.

Yes sir, I am all man. One of honor and valor,
Who does not have to hide his emotions.
Crying becomes a man of strength when
The tears are a sincere expression of love.

If you can understand my pain and my sorrow,
Come, I invite you to cry with me.
Together, in crying, we can relieve
The anguish of loneliness from our souls.

My mistake has been an expensive lesson;
Being separated from my family is my punishment.
Now, you know why my heart is broken,
So, don't judge me if sometimes I cry.

–Orlando

Chapter 6

DESIGNS

All families have a design. W.R. Beavers and his team (1977) studied families and discovered that power, emotion, communication, and goals determine the structure of a family. I have adapted Beavers' work into five common family designs. These designs (patterns) unconsciously shape the family and behavior of the children.

AUTOCRATIC DESIGN

A dictator rules the autocratic family. I call this person Cartoon because he is "fake," like a cartoon character. Cartoon is a "legend in his own mind." He imagines that he is a king, owner, and boss. He rules his family with the iron fist of criticism and fear. Cartoon is unforgiving, cold, and controlling. He is governed by his impulses and desires while other family members are expected to cater to his whims. In other words, there is a double standard; Cartoon is a hypocrite. He makes and breaks the rules but expects other family members to comply. He is feared but not liked, antisocial and aggressive.

Autocratic design families abuse children; violence is common. Cartoon may berate or beat family members into submission. Autocratic families do not discuss important matters because selfish Cartoon rarely spends time with the children except to criticize. As can be expected, he makes all the important decisions.

Cartoon's children are shamed and consequently struggle with negative (low) self-esteem. They live with internal rage and depression. The children learn to lie, bully, and fight because they have never been treated with respect. Johnny may sleep with a knife under his pillow, and he cannot wait to leave home and start his own autocratic family.

In time, Cartoon's passive children will adopt his antisocial and aggressive behavior; it is all they know. This behavior does not lead to healthy relationships and intimacy. When Cartoon was a boy, he was passive and dependent around his aggressive mother or father. Since no one taught Cartoon about intimacy, he unconsciously re-created the dysfunctional family he experienced as a child.

Abusers desperately need to relearn patterns of interaction and intimacy. However, this is very difficult because they believe that vulnerability is a sign of weakness. Therefore, they tend to abuse those who dare to love them the most.

David told me, "My dad is the only man in the world who scares me. One time he shoved me into the wall so hard it busted the wall."

HURT, HATE, AND HARM

"I have experienced hurt, hate, and harm in relation-ships in my past. But not like the hurt, hate, and harm I experienced with my father. To be perfectly honest with you, as far as I'm concerned, I had no father! He has never been there for me, nor has he ever done anything for me! Out of my whole life, he's given me one thing —a baseball glove and bat! This is my hurt, among the mental hurt I went through as a child.

I'll explain. I always felt hurt when he beat my mother. And a lot of times, I would try to help my mom and he would hit me too. I was four years old when he tried to drown my mom in the bathtub. I jumped on his back, and he kicked me down the steps. After that day, my mom packed me, and my brother and sister's things, and we left him. All I have is bad memo-ries about my father.

When he died, I felt no remorse for him. I cried because I saw my mother cry. My harm was his abuse! My hate...that's a good one. I hate that I was deprived of having a father. I hate him for abusing my mother phys-ically and his children mentally. I hate that he put up an effort in spreading his seed but didn't put up an effort to take any responsibility as a father. He would rather get high and beat my mom and steal from us than be a parent. He is the prime example of the type of man I never want to be. This is why I hate the fact that I'm incarcerated away from my children. I know what it feels like not to have a father. I'm sure my children miss me because I miss them."

–Charles

Autocratic families smother one another and unconsciously promise never to talk about the abuse. Mom makes excuses for Dad's behavior, "Your father is under a lot of pressure."

Children promise themselves, "I will never be like Dad."

We may wonder, "Why would a woman choose to marry someone like a Cartoon?" Let us remember, we unconsciously repeat the design of our past. Initially, a woman may fall for Cartoon's strength and passion. Perhaps he makes her feel secure and valued, something she may have never known. In time, the relationship becomes a trap, but by now there are children who need a home.

TRADITIONAL DESIGN

The traditional family design shares a loyalty that holds the family together. The loyalty might be tradition, family ties, location, or work. There is a clear chain of command and consequences for disloyal behavior. Dad and Mom follow traditional roles: Dad drives the car and always sits in the same chair at dinner; Mom nurtures the children and makes the house a home. Children quickly learn the roles of their gender and are expected to be obedient. Although children may rebel and wish for change, discipline maintains the traditional design.

The strength of this family is loyalty. The family conforms to established behavioral rules and roles. Holidays are celebrated with great gusto as the entire family gathers to eat, laugh, tease, and bond. Frequently, the men socialize while the women prepare the food. Older children assume responsibility for their younger brothers and sisters. Individuals sacrifice personal ambition for the sake of family. As an example, Johnny followed Papa into the family business even though he secretly hoped to become an artist.

Traditional families are healthy. Because of respect and concern, children develop positive self-esteem and become responsible, loyal, and hard working adults.

Most social institutions operate according to a traditional design not unlike the traditional family. Corporations, schools, churches, and government agencies, including prisons, all follow the traditional design and operate according to established policies and patterns. The purpose of the institution takes priority over the concerns of the individual.

INTIMATE DESIGN

The central focus of an intimate family design is communication and intimacy. There is a clear pecking order; Mom and Dad assume responsibility for the safety and wholeness of the children. Decisions are reached through discussion and consensus. Parents offer their children a lot of freedom but also challenge them to think about their actions and the social consequences.

Sharing responsibility, fun, and dreams are central to the intimate design. When the family expresses respect and appreciation, children feel secure and loved. The primary purpose of an intimate family is to prepare children for life by helping them assume responsibility and think congruently (clearly and logically). The family is a unit, bonds are evident, but others are welcome to participate, share the warmth and secrets. Discipline is a process, focused on teaching responses to life instead of creating fear and blame. The commitment to each other is balanced with a commitment to individual growth and wholeness. Members are encouraged to express their own opinions, including anger.

Intimate families are healthy; children have positive self-esteem. They learn respect, responsibility, and balance. They find meaning in relationships but strive for personal fulfillment.

PERMISSIVE DESIGN

A permissive family design is relaxed and flexible because it focuses on the unique development of each person. Early on, parents encourage their children to develop personal interests and hobbies. This leads to a strong sense of individualism and autonomy—financed by Mom and Dad. Children may not experience the closeness of an intimate family or the structure of a traditional family, but they are world citizens: bright, adept, and able.

This is a very democratic family; permissive parents tend to side with the children as readily as with one another. Blended families may adopt the permissive design because the parent/child relationship occurred before the spousal relationship.

Children of this design have high expectations. They are less sheltered than children from traditional and intimate families. They are socially adept and push the limits, becoming artists, designers, authors, musicians, and high achievers. Or, they might wander off into eccentricity, isolation, and loneliness. Discipline and restraint is minimal; children learn through social interaction. Parents see themselves as launching pads and safety nets for the children and may end up financially supporting them long after they leave home.

Permissive families are healthy. These children have high ambitions and positive self-esteem. They are self-assured almost to the point of arrogance and frequently become successful.

CHAOTIC DESIGN

At the heart of a chaotic family is chaos. There is very little structure and consistency; there is always neglect and change. Children worry about survival and safety. No one fixes breakfast, and they never know if Mom will be home when they get out of school. Chaotic children routinely live with parental neglect.

Our communities, especially our cities, have an epidemic of chaotic families. Boundaries are fragile, almost nonexistent. Chaotic children live in a "dog-eat-dog" world. There is little family commitment because members are consumed with self-interest. Few boundaries separate members of the family from visitors and friends.

This family may begin as an autocratic design and become chaotic when Dad walks out. Drugs lure parents away from children who are then left in the hands of the resident babysitter —the television. As these children are left to parent themselves, they are exposed to dope, dealing, violence, sex, and crime.

Children from chaotic families live in a borderline world. Life is about survival and self-interest. These children experience first hand the hardships of street life. Adult children of chaotic families struggle with personal discipline, intimacy, and loyalty. They have enormous egos because they have conquered enormous odds. However, no one has taught these children the beauty of trust, affection, or empathy. Chaotic adults believe, "It's better to live and trust no one, than to trust someone and get hurt." They may also believe the world owes them a living and have unrealistic

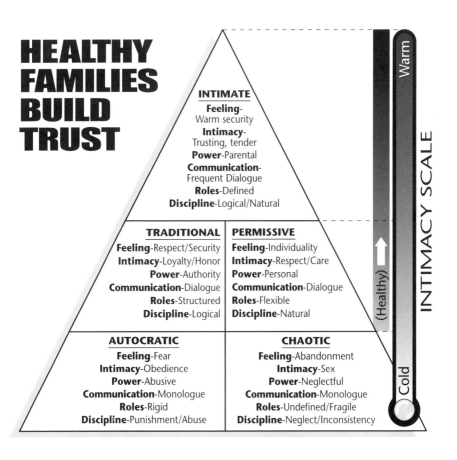

HEALTHY FAMILIES BUILD TRUST

INTIMACY SCALE

Warm · (Healthy) · Cold

INTIMATE
Feeling- Warm security
Intimacy- Trusting, tender
Power-Parental
Communication- Frequent Dialogue
Roles-Defined
Discipline-Logical/Natural

TRADITIONAL
Feeling-Respect/Security
Intimacy-Loyalty/Honor
Power-Authority
Communication-Dialogue
Roles-Structured
Discipline-Logical

PERMISSIVE
Feeling-Individuality
Intimacy-Respect/Care
Power-Personal
Communication-Dialogue
Roles-Flexible
Discipline-Natural

AUTOCRATIC
Feeling-Fear
Intimacy-Obedience
Power-Abusive
Communication-Monologue
Roles-Rigid
Discipline-Punishment/Abuse

CHAOTIC
Feeling-Abandonment
Intimacy-Sex
Power-Neglectful
Communication-Monologue
Roles-Undefined/Fragile
Discipline-Neglect/Inconsistency

expectations because they are not familiar with family life.

The preceding pyramid will help you to understand some of the differences and similarities of the five designs.

Marie told me that her family started as traditional but became permissive when her father and mother separated. What kind of family design do you have?

Healthy family designs: intimate, traditional, and permissive, excel at communication, respect, intimacy, and discipline. Dysfunctional families: autocratic and chaotic, fail to communicate, never develop trusting patterns of intimacy and resort to punishment and neglect instead of discipline.

ANYWAY

People are unreasonable, illogical, and self-centered,
LOVE THEM ANYWAY
If you do good, people will accuse you of selfish, ulterior motives,
DO GOOD ANYWAY
If you are successful, you win false friends and true enemies,
SUCCEED ANYWAY
The good you do will be forgotten tomorrow,
DO GOOD ANYWAY
Honesty and frankness make you vulnerable,
BE HONEST AND FRANK ANYWAY
What you spent years building may be destroyed overnight,
BUILD ANYWAY
People really need help but may attack you if you help them,
HELP PEOPLE ANYWAY
Give the world the best you have and you will get kicked in the teeth,
GIVE THE WORLD THE BEST YOU'VE GOT ANYWAY.

–From a sign on the wall of Shishu Bhavan,
The children's home in Calcutta

Chapter 7

DIALOGUE

Professor Martin Buber was on his way to class when a young man approached him to ask if they could talk. He agreed to give the student a few minutes. The following week, Martin Buber learned that the young man had committed suicide. This tragedy deeply affected Dr. Buber as he reflected on his interaction with the student and inspired him to write a powerful little book titled, I-THOU. Buber says we cannot be complete without each other; complete isolation ends in insanity. In other words, only through dialogue (interaction) can we be whole; the confirmation of others completes us.

"I-Thou" relationships are intimate and sacred. This is the best relationship of a mother with her child. The mother comes face to face with the personality of the child and chooses to find beauty. She is the soil from which the child grows. How can a child rebel from such affirmation and tenderness? Who wants to be freed from the womb? Fathers complete this confirmation with a voice of authority, "Come here, Son." Words of belonging seep into the hidden soul and bring identity, "My, how beautiful you are becoming, Daughter." Like a gentle hug, such words from a father drive away doubts of inadequacy. Mom and Dad must learn to affirm their child and bring out the child's beauty.

According to Buber, treating each other as an "it" (object) leads to withdrawal and disease. Affirming the unique beauty of each other (Thou) and confirming the "oneness" of the relationship (I-Thou) bring healing.

In preceding chapters, we have discussed the importance of trust, awareness, values, spirituality, and design. However, none of this matters unless we learn to talk. Incarcerated fathers must ask, "How can I best dialogue with my child and create intimacy during my imprisonment?"

MINOR

Minor sits attentively in class even though he has a difficult time understanding English. Fortunately, we have two bilingual students from New York who help Minor understand what I am saying. One afternoon, Minor hangs around after the bell. As the class empties, he signals to me, reaches into his khaki pocket, and pulls out a well-worn envelope. Minor carefully unfolds the creased letter with two pictures of his wife and three daughters. Minor's family is from Dominican Republic. He rarely calls his wife and has not seen his daughters for three years. He hopes they will be able to visit the States in April. Minor works in the prison factory and sends most of his check to his mother for the family.

During our final class Minor asks Luke to translate, "I have taken notes of everything I remember in this class. I send them to my family. We are talking about our feelings, something I did not know before. Thank you." After Luke finishes speaking for Minor, he begins to talk about his own life on the street.

"I'm a former gang boss from D.C. I never learned to respect my wife. Instead, I would tell her what to do and when to do it. I had other children that she did not know about. When she would come to see me in the visiting room, I would sit like this," Luke turned his back to us, "...and never look at her except to tell her what to do. This class has helped me be honest with my wife. I've told her about my other children, and she's agreed to get them together, so they can know each other. Now I sit like this," Luke leaned forward and looked at us intently, "...and look in her eyes. Instead of telling my wife what to do, I ask how she is doing, and how can I support her. You know, she's a smart woman. I never saw that before. I've been telling her how I feel, and it has pulled us together."

VERBAL AND NON-VERBAL COMMUNICATION

There are two types of communication: verbal and non-verbal. Verbal communication is language (words), reading, writing, singing, talking. Nonverbal communication includes art, music, harmony, dance, sound, motions, expressions, smells, touch, pictures, noise, and even silence. Social scientists tell us that seventy percent (70%) of all communication is nonverbal.

In the mid-50's, a group of psychotherapists studying communication at Palo Alto, California, discovered the "double-bind" concept. In "double-bind" communication, there is a conflict between the words and tone. I call this "crossed" communication. For example, when I asked Lamar, who is "short", whether he would go "straight" when he is released, he said, "Yeah! Right! I owe the government 1.4 million dollars and I'm broke. You figure it out."

Although Lamar is saying, "Yeah!" with his words, he is saying, "No way!" with his tone. Communication occurs on two levels: words and feelings. When words and feelings clash, we have "crossed" communication, and we do not know whether to follow the words or the feelings. Congruent (healthy) people strive for clear communication (making words and feelings say the same thing). Except for play and teasing, I encourage parents to be congruent (healthy) with their child because this improves her understanding. Crossed communication is confusing.

Suppose a staff officer jokes with you, "You are on your way to the 'hole,' Buddy!" Even though the officer is joking, his words imply that you could be going to solitary confinement. As you see, crossed communication can be very stressful and is not helpful unless the message is clearly offered in play and jest.

I roll up a newspaper and run around the house yelling, "I'm tired of this." I act angry as I chase my daughters with the newspaper, but they know that I am teasing because we have played this game before. "I'm sick and tired of the way you...you...you make good grades and clean your room." My daughters squeal and run. They lock themselves in the bathroom. When I finally catch them, we tussle and laugh. Then they take the newspaper and tear into me.

WORDS AS SYMBOLS

Words are symbols. For example, consider the word "tie." What does "tie" mean? Necktie? Railroad tie? Tie score? Tie a knot?

"Tie" is a symbol that jumps to the brain for any one of a dozen explanations (pictures). The only way to understand the meaning of "tie" is to understand how it fits in the conversation. When I say, "I need a tie for the trash bag," the brain knows exactly how to interpret "tie."

Sooner or later every class argues over the meaning of a word. I have heard arguments about God, sex, values, faith, intimacy, and countless other words. If we can learn that words are symbols, the argument ends. The symbol is only a word picture, pointing to a reality beyond. Try to understand words (pictures) from the other person's perspective.

LEVELS TO INTIMACY

Conversation becomes warm and fun when it leaves the cold, rational world and bubbles with the passions of the heart. Would you rather hear Kimberly say, "It's such a nice day!" or "I really miss you and need you!" Feelings add warmth to conversation and make it more delightful. There are various levels to intimate conversation: banter, discussion, dialogue, and empathetic dialogue.

BANTER

The first level of conversation is banter: "Hey, what's up?" "Yo!" "How's it going?" These are the first small steps to dialogue. Banter eases our social interaction.

DISCUSSION

Discussion is more mental and factual than banter; it involves thinking and tracking. We might think of discussion as "mind to mind" conversation. When someone selects a topic, members either track with the discussion or introduce another topic. Discussion is the exchange of factual, objective information:

"Did you see the Penn State game?"

"Yeah, but right now I'm pulling for U.K. They are awesome this year."

Anyway, you get the picture. Discussion is the exchange of objective information that involves thinking.

DIALOGUE

Dialogue adds feelings and therefore warmth to discussion. With dialogue, smiles break out, and the conversation becomes less formal and more relaxed. Dialogue has the potential to heal us, which is the point of therapy. Human beings hunger for this level of interaction, eye to eye, heart to heart, soul to soul.

Make no mistake, dialogue is more than talk; it is an interactive relationship that deepens intimacy. Dialogue includes gentle teasing, laughter, and sorrow. In dialogue, the old maxim is true, "I don't care how much you know until I know how much you care."

EMPATHETIC DIALOGUE

Intense dialogue is at the heart of intimacy, empathy, and compassion. Feeling words such as hurt, fear, alone, cry, embarrassed, touch, important, love, happy, sorry, yes, surprise, trust, dream, wonderful, and welcome begin to season our language. We create room for the other person in our heart; we listen, we smile, we hold, we care, we protect, we touch, we love. Empathetic dialogue is not about blame, but restoration. It is not about greed, but sharing. It is not about abuse, but dignity.

Gentlemen, many fathers never get to the level of empathetic dialogue with their children. Let's face it, men would rather cry with their dog than with their family. We know how to tease, head butt, break wind, and live off dirt, but cuddling and sharing warm, fuzzy feelings with the family is extremely difficult. Can you imagine Dirty Harry being soft and intimate? Much of our conversation with our children is routine. For instance, "How'd you do in school?" or "Take out the trash," or "I can't make the game tonight."

Sharing our feelings, hopes, dreams and secrets is the deepest level of conversation. We must learn about these "matters of the heart" from those we love. Dialogue never ends; I must continually hear my children's dreams and sorrow as they hear mine. If I want their love, I had better accept their hurt. When fathers block feelings, they block intimacy. Now, I am certainly not suggesting that our first words to Junior should be, "What scares you, Son?" But until we learn to talk with our sons, how will they learn to talk with their sons, our grandsons? Since it is difficult to talk about love, start with, "I miss you; I really enjoy talking with you."

Dialogue brings intimacy. Like a bank account, members invest in one another and that helps carry them through times of crisis and conflict. Remember, not all dialogue is verbal. In fact, close families share many non-verbal cues. Genuine smiles, laughter, and tenderness are non-verbal ways to build lasting intimacy. During a visit, look intently at your child and smile. In a matter of seconds she will look at you and say, "What?" Tell her how much you enjoy knowing her and being her dad. By the way, women interpret nonverbal signals much better than men do.

Daryl wrote to his daughter Judi, hoping that his angry ex would give her the letter. After writing six letters and hearing nothing, Daryl wanted to give up. I asked him if he had a six-week commitment to Judi. I encouraged him to help with her expenses and talk as positively as possible about Mom. Three months after Daryl started writing, he received a letter. In a few more weeks, Judi asked him to call. Now Daryl writes regularly and calls her on special occasions. He has made peace with his ex for Judi's sake. A child never wins when she is caught between Mom and Dad.

It will take time to mend the hurt and bitterness of a neglected child. However, connecting with your child will help her deal with unresolved anger and begin to find healing. Too many fathers do not help with the support of their children. This puts the child at a disadvantage and gives your ex a reasonable gripe. Supporting your child, just a little each month, will help your child feel valued and ease the resentment of your ex. It is important to celebrate birthdays and special days with your child.

Please do not play with your child's heart. She needs you. She needs your protection and love. The greatest responsibility of a man is fatherhood.

STYLES OF COMMUNICATION

Virginia Satir, an early pioneer working with families, discovered five ways we respond to one another during communication. **Placater:** According to Satir, the placater is a "yes" person. Afraid of conflict, this person always agrees. "Whatever you decide will be okay with me."

Blamer: The blamer's favorite word is "you"..."It's your fault." This person seeks a scapegoat because he is too fragile to accept responsibility. It is easier to blame than seek a solution.

Computer: The computer person is only interested in the facts. Husbands tend to communicate this way. "Honey, just give me the facts, will you?" A "computer" offers answers and solutions but does not offer dialogue and warmth. He is cool and detached.

Distracter: The distracter seems unable to relate to the conversation. This person will distract others with a wisecrack to avoid meaningful dialogue. Distracters are evasive and difficult to pin down.

Leveler: The "leveler" is a straight shooter. He is real, genuine, and mature enough to send clear, simple messages. The leveler is balanced and able to deal with emotion. Inner peace allows him to listen. He responds to the situation instead of creating a situation.

"I" MESSAGES

The best way to communicate is with "I" messages. "I" messages express our feelings about a specific situation and imply an acceptance of responsibility. For example, "I feel unimportant when I think you are not listening to me."

Too often, in the heat of an argument, we use "you" language along with "never" and "always." Phil told Wanda, "You are never home when I call. You are always over at your mother's." Wanda immediately feels like she must play defense.

Phil might have said, "I get bummed when I call, and you're not home."

Len yells at his cellie, "You always leave the door open. Close the door."

Instead, Len might say, "I get frustrated when you leave the door open because all the neighborhood thieves sneak into our cell and steal the toilet paper. Close the door."

"I" messages are about how I feel and why I feel the way I do. These messages are not about blame but vulnerability and honesty.

DIALOGUE FROM JAIL

Letters, visits, and telephone calls are ways to communicate with your family from prison. I realize that fathers in prison play with a handicap; it is not easy to find the strength to build intimacy. But I know men who have better relationships with their children from jail than they ever had on the street. The isolation of prison can teach men about their need for intimacy.

LETTERS

Letters give loved ones something valuable to hold and to keep. Holly sleeps with her father's letters under her pillow; Justin carries them around in his pocket. Letters are wonderful keepsakes because they are tangible (real). Children grasp a letter from their father like a life preserver. They reread the letter because they are starved for a father's love. If the child does not understand the letter, he can save it for a later time. It is most important that you write to your children a couple times each month.

I encourage fathers to send art and pictures for their children to color. Develop some basic art skills and send special cards and letters during the holidays. Send five-year-old Ellyn a maze, seven-year-old Jon math problems, and ten-year-old Justin drawings of the Bulls team. If Justin loves the team, send him a hand drawn card of each player, so he can collect the team. Rita might enjoy word games and puzzles that you have designed. Read the books that your children are reading, so you can share the stories. Draw pictures of your children, of your room, or of the things you miss. Draw a picture of Rita in ten years; put a graduation cap on her head. Art is a wonderful way to communicate with children.

Teenagers appreciate stories and affirmation. Many men ask me to write a letter to their child. The following is a sample letter for a young teenage son:

Dear Shark (Lee),

I'm gonna start calling you Shark because you have a wonderful smile and plenty of teeth. As I looked at your picture this week, I found myself wondering how I am so blessed to have a son like you. I really never knew my father, and I missed some of my chance to know you. Now I realize how important you are to me and I don't want to miss out like my father. You know, I've made some big, huge, really dumb mistakes but not when I fathered you. I'm taking a parenting class, and today I showed my class your last letter and how I carry it around in my pocket. It's getting kinda worn from all my reading and sitting on it, but it's one of my most precious possessions, and I'm gonna keep it there till you write again, and I can replace it.

Son, I am happy you're interested in sports. You got a lot of potential and natural ability. Sports seem to come easy to you. Just do me a favor, zone down on the math homework. Last time I talked to your mother, she said you were studying hard but a little frustrated with math. I'm on my way to the library to check out a math book to try and learn with you. Next time we talk, I want you to teach me about what you're learning.

Hey, Shark, you are becoming a man. I can see how your mother has been solid for you. You carry her beauty in your heart.

I did want to tell you about Uncle Willy. He used to live behind us when we lived on Pratt Street, and I was about your age. I remember the time he loaded me up in his old truck, and we spent the weekend moving your Aunt Thelma and Uncle James to Brooklyn. I never knew what to talk about, but old Uncle Willy and I had a good time. He told me back then that I had potential, but I was afraid to believe him. You got that same potential and more.

Okay, I'm gonna cut this short and write again soon. Look for a green shark on the envelope. I do want to hear from you. Your letters really brighten up my week...I mean my life. Tell me what you're doing in math, and I will look it up, so you can teach me. I miss you, Son. There's not a night that I don't suffer 'cause we're apart. I love you, Lee.

Love, Dad

OMAR

Omar asked me about ways to build intimacy with his son Robert. The following week Omar came to class with a wonderful story about the adventures of Colonel O and Captain Rob. Captain Rob is the good Colonel's right-hand man. The chapter ended with Captain Rob in an elevator with three choices. He can escape to the laundry room, the helicopter pad, or the subway. The button that young Robert pushes will become the beginning of a new chapter. Each week Omar plans to draw pictures and write another chapter about the adventures of Captain Rob. Each episode ends with Robert choosing the next adventure. What a creative way to make a child feel valued!

Lobo collects postage stamps from mail that comes to his friends from all over the world. On his son's birthday Lobo sent him a book of stamps. With pride Lobo told me how his son took the gift to school to show classmates.

Stay connected with your children through interactive hobbies, games, stories, collections, art, et cetera. Develop an interactive detective game and provide clues. For instance, what is the connection between Enrico Fermi and the Enola Gay? Think of creative projects to be involved in the life of your children.

LISTENING

Communication, especially dialogue, includes listening. If I talk to you with words that you cannot understand, we have not fully communicated. When we send a signal into space, we have not communicated unless someone picks up that signal and responds. Dialogue is giving and receiving, talking and listening.

Very few people know how to listen, especially to children. Listening is more than knowing what someone might say; it is hearing their feelings. Parents who fail to hear their children are setting the stage for misbehavior because every child must release his enthusiasm, fear, and frustration. Failure to listen creates disobedience. On the other hand, careful listening will build respect and allow the child to release excitement, frustration, and hurt through verbal expression.

LISTENING GUIDE: I-N-Q-U-I-R-E

I = *Express Interest.*
N = *Look for non-verbal cues.*
Q = *Ask questions.*
U = *Measure your feelings.*
I = *Make "I" statements, make eye contact.*
R = *Respond at the same level of affection.*
E = *Do not forget empathy.*

VISITS

Visits are wonderful opportunities to see and touch those you love. I realize that hugs and kisses are not always allowed. Enjoy the eyes of the ones you love; there is magic. Look for your reflection, and learn that every smile is a mirror of your beauty. Commit the smile to memory; it is for you. Do not miss the signs of affection from your family. Talk about things that are important for the relationship to grow and deepen.

I encourage families to take turns visiting Dad. Plan to spend one visit with the children and the next with the spouse. It is difficult for spouses to visit if children are jealous and want attention.

CRITICISM, BLAME, CONTROL

Just as positive dialogue builds intimacy, negative interaction tears it apart. Criticism, blame, and control will eventually destroy a relationship. Parents sometimes criticize their child, "Stop that!" "You're not being good." "Get over here and quit bothering those people." Instead of looking for opportunities to bless and encourage, parents end up scolding the child. This kind of negative parenting is unhealthy and destructive. Ask the child to help you develop a game. Use the tiles on the floor for tic-tac-toe. See who can sit quietly for five minutes without saying anything. Plan for their visit by imagining activities that will help you be together as a family. Healthy parents seek opportunities to encourage and affirm.

Chapter 8

INTIMACY

Few topics, at least in a male prison, are more delightful than discussions about women. Men enjoy talking about women, learning about women, being near women, and knowing women. We have a natural desire to be accepted and loved by women. Incarcerated men quickly learn to enjoy the soft scent of a woman's perfume hanging in the air.

DATING

Have you ever thought about the ritual of dating? We have all watched animals perform mating rituals, perhaps via television. But when we stop to think about it, humans also have rituals, not just for dating but for all interactions.

Romance is planted in us long before the first date. Early on we are teased about liking a certain girl. Over the years we find ourselves wondering, what is he like, what is she like? We enjoy learning about the opposite sex.

In my culture, we initiate a date by making a little eye contact, but not too much. Whenever we intrude into a stranger's emotional space, we must be careful not to enter too quickly, or we threaten that person. Next, we engage in a slight gesture of acknowledgement such as a wave or nod. This might be followed with our best line and humor. If that goes well, we could end up exchanging phone numbers.

On our first phone call, we make light conversation before inviting her to an activity. The first date is a non-threatening event, a ball game, movie, or dinner. We are courteous and respectful. Slowly, we increase eye and body contact. The conversation becomes more personal as we talk about our work or family. During a movie, he may drape his arm over her shoulder and whisper, "You look pretty." We acknowledge our attraction, possibly through touch.

We have cultural norms for entering another person's body space. We do it slowly through the invitation of nonverbal cues. A verbal rejection probably means that we have misread the nonverbal signs. Dating etiquette allows the relationship to grow without fear. If the man begins to pressure the woman, he breaks the rules of etiquette, and she may end the date. Manners are important because they help people relate with ease. Ronald Johnson says, "Manners will take you where money never will."

Assuming the nonverbal cues are encouraging, the man may offer her his arm or she may reach for his hand. At this point, both persons understand the relationship is moving toward intimacy.

The interactive ritual to this point has included eye to eye, voice to voice, phone to phone, step to step, nonverbal cues to nonverbal cues, and arm to arm or hand to hand. The dance continues....

When he takes her home, she may wait for him to drop a clue. She may linger for a moment in the car or invite him to come in for some coffee. He may move to hug her, neck to neck, or kiss her softly and promise to call.

Lip to lip suggests both persons believe the relationship is a romance. As the relationship deepens, eye to eye contact increases along with feelings, touching, and increased physical intimacy. Can you see the slow unfolding of intimacy? Slowly, as we learn to trust, barriers are dropped and intimacy grows.

A man may want to jump the gun and have sexual intercourse before his partner feels safe. This undermines the relationship and respect.

Ellis waited excitedly for his first twelve-hour furlough. His wife decorated the motel room, and they drove right from prison to the motel where Ellis forced himself on his wife. He told me later that it ruined the day. She wanted to talk and open her heart; Ellis wanted to unzip his pants. Ellis wanted to go genital to genital before going heart to heart.

CHAIRS

I can arrange the chairs in my class, but when the men enter the classroom, they push the chairs around to give themselves more space. Men are uncomfortable being close, especially with other men. When we hug, we pat each other on the back as if to say, "It's okay, I'm not being turned on by this hug."

We are paranoid about our sexuality. We talk about women as if they are body parts because we have never become comfortable talking about ourselves. No wonder so many women obsess with being thin, or young, or sexy—that is what men are buying. Ouch! We know how to admire our lady's beauty, but we have never learned to admire her strength. We know how to talk about her, but we have never learned to talk with her. We know how to win, but we have never learned how to play.

Head butts, secret signs, high-fives, and grunting, Tim "Toolman" Taylor style, are intimate responses among men. We approach sexual intercourse like football. Hit 'em good, hit 'em hard, and let 'em lay. We are intimate, and I use the word loosely, for the performance but then retreat because of the intensity of closeness. It seems like our hormones throw us together, and we almost wish we could have the sexual pleasure without such proximity.

CARLOS

Carlos would lift weights before coming to class. He used to tell me, "Lifting weights and running like a crazy man releases my anger." I remember asking him, "Does lifting and running really release your anger or just exhaust you physically?" Carlos smiled.

Men approach sex like Carlos approaches exercise, interested in the payoff, not the process. Sexual intercourse is a quick fix, but it will never satisfy our unconscious hunger for nurture and unconditional love. If women do not experience intimacy during sexual intercourse, they feel the man is a sexual intruder.

INTIMACY

Intimacy is about vulnerability, risk, and commitment. As we learned at the beginning, intimacy comes from trust. As trust deepens, friends take off their masks to share their hurt and hope, fears and dreams.

Intimacy is love without pretense; it is the warm embrace of unconditional nurture. Intimacy is not about sex, marriage, or touch. It is a joining of hearts. For too many men, this is difficult; sex is as close as we get. Where did we learn that the goal of intimacy is sex? We have it backward; the goal of sex is intimacy. Intimacy releases our creative power. In the hour of creation there is unity and oneness, hearts melted in the fiery embrace—hopefully, of love.

The organ of intimacy is the eye, not the penis. Try looking into the eyes of those you love. It will light you up! Eye to eye intimacy is inspiring and enduring.

BIG AL

Big Al sat in the back of the class and poked fun anytime we talked about feelings. I remember him saying, "I don't go for all that mushy stuff." When I asked the class for homework, he brought in a poem. I told him it was excellent and asked him to share it with the class. The men responded so favorably that Big Al sent the poem to his wife. The following week he came to see me and told me that his wife loved it.

"That's great!" I said.

"No, Mr. Wolfgang, you don't understand." Something in Big Al's voice grabbed my attention, and I saw tears in his eyes. "For the first time since we've been together, my wife told me that she loved me; it's been eight years." Not surprisingly, Big Al learned the value of feelings and became the class poet.

The fool is thirsty in the midst of water.
Ethiopian proverb

JULIE LYNN

I have been here for quite some time,
And I can't stop the things that go through my mind;
Remembering the times that I was free,
Holding hands just you and me.
I can't forget the love that we have shared,
And all the times it seemed I did not care.
I truly believe you were sent from above,
And I thank God for sending this love.
Without you, I would not be whole;
You are the one that fills up my soul.
I look forward to when I'll return.
To sleep in your bed is all that I yearn.
To be with my family and live as one,
This is my one wish under the sun.
For you are my only, above any sin,
The woman I love and married; it's you Julie Lynn.

–Big Al

FAMILY INTIMACY

Intimacy is vital to our family's emotional health. Trust builds intimacy, which creates value and esteem. Children need our protection, our understanding, our respect, and our affection. If neglect and abuse cause suffering and despair, intimacy is the secret of wholeness. Build a bond of trust with your child, in the process, you will find yourself becoming whole. Women have an advantage of learning about intimacy through motherhood. If you have never experienced a warm, safe family, it will be difficult to understand the depth of warmth and security an intimate family offers a child. But every heart deserves this kind of confirmation, for it completes us.

RELAXATION

Relaxation is critical for intimacy. The first step in relaxation is surrender. Find a place where you feel safe, and allow yourself to be comfortable. Slowly relax the muscles in your body. Focus on breathing. Relax your body. Inhale...count to four, and exhale. Again, inhale...count to four, and exhale.

Now, create an imaginary place of beauty and peace. Water may be used to add serenity. Place yourself in the picture. What do you see? Take time to relax, and look around at the image you are creating. What do you hear? Feel? Smell?

Affirm yourself, "I will allow myself to be loved and nurtured. I will give myself peace." Once you are resting quietly, ask, "How do I feel inside? What do I need? Why do I need to visit this peaceful place?" Involve your senses and your feelings. As you listen and look, feel your inner peace. Enjoy the warmth and your memory. Explore your awareness.

Until we are peaceful, we cannot embrace those we love and be intimate. Imagine you are with a friend. What is she saying with her silence? What is he feeling? When it is time to talk, speak about what you feel in your heart. Listen without becoming defensive. Intimacy is not about judgment and correction but understanding and acceptance. Listen, and others will listen to you.

Near the end of your visit, plan to return to your special place. Now, slowly return to reality bringing the serenity of your experience.

FAMILY MEETINGS

Family meetings are wonderful ways to clear the air, set goals, work at discipline, reinforce behavior, and encourage children. Grades, holidays, concerns, crisis, finances, and celebrations are all reasons to gather the family and talk. At our home, anyone can call a family meeting. We use the meetings to affirm and encourage one another. We might plan a vacation or tell the family what we hope to get for our birthday. We meet when the children get their report cards to celebrate and challenge them. If we believe our child can do better in school, we ask, "What can I do to help you bring up your grade in math?" This year we even dared to prioritize our finances at the family meeting. Pam and I believe this will be good financial experience for our children. We agreed to fix the hall and help Angi with her tuition; next year we hope to visit Jamaica. My family encouraged me to write this book and made adjustments to give me the time. They celebrate with me the completion of each chapter and together we hope and dream.

Everyone is expected to participate at a family meeting. Take time to ask each child, "What do you think about this?" We meet to discuss behavior problems and even my need to control the remote. I ask my family to hold me accountable to be a good father. Yesterday my daughter said, "Dad, I want you to vacuum the house, do some wash, and collect the trash." There are times when we yell and times when we cry. I remember one evening when we took turns clapping for each other. We have shared our hurts and fears. We have laughed and poked fun at each other. Through it all, we talk, we care.

We have met in the car, in the living room, at the kitchen table, during a walk, and on a blanket at the beach. I encourage my students to meet in the visiting room, preferably on a day when the room is not crowded. Family meetings teach respect.

HOT SEAT

Ande started it on the day he said, "Now we tell about the Wolfman." Near the end of each class, I assert the executive power that belongs to every teacher, and I place each student on the "hot seat." For approximately ten minutes, the class focuses their attention and comments on this person. Thoughtfully, the men speak about the selected individual. We have two rules: focus on the person on the hot seat; and, make it positive. Anyone who breaks the rules is bumped up—next on the hot seat. Students are often surprised by the profound insight of the other students. For too many men, I sense this is the first time anyone took the time to look at them deeply and say something positive.

Put members of your family on the hot seat during visiting hours. Start with an adult, so children can learn the rules. If you do the hot seat routine often enough, you will find that complimenting one another becomes a wonderful part of your family life.

QUALITIES OF A HEALTHY FAMILY

FREEDOM FROM FEAR.
Freedom from fear builds wholeness.

AFFECTION.
Warm, tender affection builds respect and intimacy.

MUTUAL COMMITMENT.
Commitment provides glue for the difficult times.

I NTIMATE DIALOGUE.
Communication brings openness and clarity.

LAUGHTER/PLAY.
Like sunlight, happiness lifts the spirit.

YIELDING EMPATHY.
Empathy brings understanding and tenderness.

F-A-M-I-L-Y leads to intimacy and wholeness. Gentlemen, although you are playing with a handicap, you can accomplish every one of these goals from prison.

DREAMS

Intimate families dream together. Sometimes, the only way to get through today is to have hope for tomorrow. I tell my daughters, "You are now the future of this family. Everything past now comes to dance in you; everything future now comes from you. I am looking forward to the day when you will make me a grandfather."

The eyes of my children glisten when I tell them how important their dreams and families will be to me. I want to become the old man in my family and show the youngsters how to age with integrity.

Healthy families spend time together at regular intervals. Commitment and encouragement are reaffirmed during these moments of solidarity. If the unspoken rules of a dysfunctional family are **SHUT UP; SHUT OUT; and SHUT DOWN**; then the rules of an intimate family are **TALK; FEEL; and CARE!**

DIRECTION

Incarcerated fathers ask, "How can I direct my child? I certainly haven't set a good example. I mean, look at me."

I respond, "You can be a good father because you have been there: you know the temptations your children will face. Challenge them to learn from your mistakes."

When your son refuses to talk to you, he is communicating with his silence. Silence and withdrawal are signs of unresolved anger. Value your child enough to understand his anger. It is the responsibility of a father to initiate communication and protect the child. Anticipate the concerns of your child and stand by to deal with those concerns. With young children this will be difficult. Young children have enough to do, just to get through the day. They do not lie around and think about Daddy in jail. However, I would encourage you to make a habit of remembering him during a certain time of the day, perhaps every evening at eleven o'clock. Write to your child, and tell him that you look at his picture or pray for him daily. Watch a favorite television program together, then write about it. Draw her favorite cartoon characters, and send them home for the child to color. Create a story, and put your child in the middle of the plot. Draw pictures of images that he enjoys. Keep the covenant with your child; this gives him value, which is the best gift a father can offer.

For teenage children, study and do research. I realize many incarcerated fathers feel helpless, but with a little creativity and commitment there is so much you can do for your child. Teenagers need mentors, not dictators. Be alert to the issues confronting your son. For example, if you have access to newspapers from all over the nation, help him with a school report by gathering information. Become an expert on punctuation, and allow him to read his reports over the phone as you help him learn. Teach her about the job market and the stock market. Help your son consider his future by listening to his dreams and desires. Research vocations and colleges. Learn all you can about computers, and encourage your children to take computer classes. Incarcerated fathers can have wonderful relationships with their children. Find other committed fathers, and ask how they are making the relationship grow. You can do it.

With adult children, write about memories of your family. Encourage them. Ask them how you can help. Ask for permission to write to your grandchildren. Talk about the good memories of family life. Read the newspaper, and bring important information to their attention through a letter.

Learning to know your child is a beautiful accomplishment that will bring deep joy.

TRIBUTE TO A WOMAN

A woman is the most beautiful of all creation; God bequeaths in her His highest inspiration. She is fragile, delicate as the soft petal of a flower. She's the discrete fragrance of an enchanting aroma. A woman is tender, sweet and full of splendor. Her allurements, her figure, are like a consuming flame. Her gifts are emanations of beauty and blessing, deserving love, respect and understanding. Because of a woman, we live adorned with fantasy. It is not right to judge her, without justice or reason. Some may be bad, but it isn't the fault of the Giver. Perhaps they are only victims without love. Who more than a woman knows what is pain; who can define with certainty what is courage? Ask a mother what she feels in her heart when her womb bursts asunder with the fruit of love. A woman is the reason for a man's triumphant struggle, his desire to give her the best life offers. A mother is a queen, deserving pure attention; a sister, wife or daughter needs to be loved with devotion. A woman will always be worthy of admiration. She is one of the most precious prizes a man can win. Because of a woman, I become a dream filled poet. Because of a woman, I live and die to love her fervently.

–Orlando

Chapter 9

DISCIPLINE

Discipline builds character. The word discipline is a derivative of disciple, which means student or learner. Good discipline helps children learn respect and conflict resolution skills. By the way, "good discipline" is an oxymoron; discipline is good.

One of the toughest responsibilities of a good parent is effectively disciplining a child. Discipline is not humiliating and painful, that is punishment. Discipline is not resentment and ridicule, that is retaliation. Discipline is not violent and hostile, that is abuse. Discipline is teaching. A good way to tell whether an action is discipline or punishment is to gauge its effect on the child. Punishment creates fear and pain. Discipline encourages your child to learn and understand.

Tony said, "Yes, but sometimes my son needs a swift kick in the pants."

We all know people who think that punishment is the secret of morality. Is that true? Do prisons rehabilitate? No! Punishment creates fear and increases aggression, even though it is intended to limit violent behavior. What happens when fear ceases to be an effective restraint and rage remains? Fathers who kick their sons are promoting a cycle and driving the unwanted behavior underground. I understand there are times when talking to your child is not enough. However, there are ways to set limits and boundaries without resorting to punishment.

MARK

Mark came over to me after the class on discipline and said, "My son does drugs and I'm afraid my daughter is following his steps. Five years ago, we found some dope in Hal's room, and I knocked the "stuffing" out of him. Hal soon moved out, and we hardly ever see him. Now I see the same thing happening to my daughter, and I don't know what to do."

Mark is heartbroken and afraid of losing his children. Sadly, no one ever taught him how to spend time with Hal and Marilyn. Instead, Mark interacted negatively with his children, repeating the pattern of his father. Hal was out the door long before he moved out of the house. Dad lost his son because he never found him. "Knocking the stuffing" out of Hal was a desperate attempt to fix something that might have been corrected long ago, with intimacy. Now Mark is afraid of losing Marilyn.

Troubled children often have parents who have never learned intimacy. When children get into trouble, frantic parents drag them to a therapist and say, "Here, fix Hal and Marilyn." As parents we need to realize that Hal and Marilyn are reflections of our own pain. Delinquent behavior stems from lack of intimacy. Developing intimacy is the secret of a healthy family.

REASONS FOR MISBEHAVIOR:

1). **Lack of Affection:** Children are jealous and need to know that they are important to Mom and Dad. If they are not getting the affection or attention they want, youngsters may act out their disappointment.

   I see this in the visiting room. As Dad is talking with someone, his little daughter is looking at him and yelling. Or, the son is picking a fight with another child. Both of these children want to be treated special and valued.

   Adolescents become gang members to find the affection of a family.

2). **Hurt:** When children are hurt, they strike out to release the anger.

   Years ago, Aunt Louise gave me a small bag of Hershey candy. Jay grabbed the bag, locked himself in the bathroom and ate every piece. I was hurt and angry that Jay could so easily take something away from me. Can you believe I still remember this after thirty years? I felt like knocking the stuffing out of Jay.

Obviously, that bag of candy meant a lot to me, probably because it was a sign of Aunt Louise's affection.

3). **Fear:** Whenever we feel threatened, lost, or out of control, our natural reaction is fight or flight. Children do not know how to control fear, so they act out their emotions in anger and frustration.

4). **Modeling:** Children model the behavior they observe from adults, friends, and television. I remember riding in the car with my father and resting my arm on the open window, just like Dad. Actually, my arm barely reached the window so I rested my hand on the window.

Through observation we learn to drive a car, play basketball, cook, tell jokes, et cetera. Children repeat the behavior imprinted in their memory.

Television is so deeply rooted in the fabric of our culture that it is difficult to measure its pervasive influence. However, children who watch two to four hours of television a day will see 8,000 murders and 100,000 acts of violence by the time they have completed elementary school (Eron, L.D. 1993. Cited in DeAngelis, T. 1993, It's back: TV violence, concern for kid viewers. APA Monitor, 24 (8), p. 16). Please, turn off the television, and develop the creative potential of your children through hobbies.

GOOD PARENTS DISCIPLINE...
WITH CONSEQUENCES, INSTEAD OF PUNISHMENT.

Teach your child the consequences of his actions. Consequences may be natural or logical. Natural consequences are those that occur naturally. For example, if you brush your teeth, you will have fewer cavities. Or, if you leave your bicycle outside, it might get stolen.

Logical consequences are consequences that are paired with behavior. For instance, if you study, you will make good grades. Or, if you work, you will earn wages. Parents can pair logical consequences with the behavior that they want to accomplish; "Robin,

if you clean your room by dinner, you may visit Chris this evening."
Or, "If you finish your homework, you may watch television."

Consequences are more effective when they are stated
positively as in the preceding example. It is less effective to say,
"If you don't clean your room by dinner time, you cannot visit
Chris this evening."

CONSISTENTLY.

Consistent discipline is important because it teaches a child
boundaries. Think about seat belts. Today it is the law that we
must wear seat belts, and small children must ride in a safety
seat. If we make our children buckle up some of the time, but
not all the time, they become confused. Parents must be consistent so children learn parental expectations. Decide what is
important and what is trivial; establishing priorities teaches values.
If you allow an exception to the rule, explain why you are not
following the rule this time, so the child can understand.
Consistency is very important to training your child.

TENDERLY AND LOGICALLY.

Approach the situation like an adult; do not argue with your
child. Set fair guidelines that you expect your child to follow, and
establish consequences if the guidelines are not followed. Try to
be logical. For instance, if your child does not eat, you do not
need to send him to his room. Hunger will eventually remind
the child to reconsider his defiance. However, do not reward your
child by taking him to McDonald's.

Whenever possible, think of discipline that is a consequence
of the child's behavior. For example, if your child kicks people,
you may choose to make her wear soft slippers. If he throws his
toy truck, take the truck for awhile.

Parents may deny young children something they want, such
as time playing outside, or a favorite toy. With teenagers it is
more effective to deny a privilege, such as sleeping over at a
friend's house or watching a special show on television.

FAIRLY.

Before you discipline your child, listen to his point of view. Then, discipline him so he understands your reaction. Fairness will develop respect and prevent an attitude of revenge. You also have the right to seek outside opinions when you are not sure of an appropriate response.

BOUNDARIES

Like fences, boundaries help a child feel safe. Think about it this way, life begins as a cell, confined to a mother's womb. In time, we graduate to a crib and playpen. Before long we have run of the house and yard. Teenagers play in the neighborhood and enjoy street life. At some point, we attend high school and go downtown. As we mature, we push the boundaries outward. This process not only happens physically, but also mentally through education, emotionally through our relationships, and spiritually through our understanding. Slowly we grow beyond yesterday's fences. Hopefully, this process continues during adulthood.

Life must be experienced at a manageable pace. Experiencing too much, too quickly, may overwhelm a child and cause him to withdraw in fear. Limits and consistent rules keep a child from feeling stressed and help him deal with life. But children are not alone; prisoners tell me that the first night in jail is the worst. Overwhelming uncertainty causes this stress.

On the other hand, boundaries may be so restrictive and punitive that they encourage rebellion. As incarcerated men well know, confinement to a small space leads to regression and anger. A prisoner must reach beyond the barriers with his mind. Children who feel confined and smothered will rebel or live with depression.

Parents have the enormous challenge of deciding when to hang on and when to let go. We must be patient and help each child understand life in manageable, bite size portions, without smothering her. Teaching him to handle his freedom responsibly is the goal of discipline.

JOEY

A few years ago Joey came to live with us. Although Joey was seven years old, emotionally and mentally he was about three. Imagine a second grader's energy coupled with the mind of a three-year-old.

I promised Joey we would go swimming, so we packed our gear and headed to the pool. Several times during the afternoon Joey asked me, "Can I go off there?" He pointed to the low diving board and the happy children jumping into the water.

"No, Joey. The water is too deep at that end of the pool," I said.

Like a normal boy, Joey did not leave it alone. He asked me three times in ten minutes to jump off the dive. I finally agreed because Joey could not understand my explanation.

Joey ran excitedly to the end of the line to wait his turn. Every time another child jumped off the dive into the water, he turned to me and laughed expectantly. Finally, it was Joey's turn. Without a thought, he climbed the three steps onto the dive, smiled broadly, and unhesitatingly ran right off the end.

The first time Joey bobbed up he was no longer smiling. At this point Joey was lost, overwhelmed by the deep water and fear. I grabbed his arm and pulled him toward me as his arms flew around my neck in panic. I pushed him onto the ladder, and he jumped out of the pool.

When I caught my breath, I asked, "Joey, would you like to jump again?"

He shook his head, "No way! There's no floor!"

Joey felt lost (stressed) when he pushed beyond his limit. Children test limits; it expands their world. As parents, we try to insulate them from danger, a demanding task. Neglected children suffer deeply because no one teaches them the limits. When they jump into the pool, it is not a friend helping them out, but the lifeguard. Sadly, one day it might be the police.

WORDS

Today I said,
"Clean your room right now."
I failed to say,
"Thank you for doing a neat job."
Today I said,
"Hurry up, you are late."
I failed to say,
"I enjoy having you around."
Today I said,
"How in the world did you tear your jeans?"
I failed to say,
"You are more important to me than things."
Today I said,
"Look at this mess!"
I failed to say,
"I like the way you share with friends."
Today I said,
"Do not talk so loud."
I failed to say,
"Your ideas are important to me."
Today I said,
"Do not forget to empty the trash."
I failed to say,
"You accept responsibility well."
Today I said,
"I wish you would stop that silly giggling."
I failed to say,
"I am glad you are so happy today."
Today I said,
"Have you finished your homework?"
I failed to say,
"I am glad you do your best."
Today I said,
"I am too busy."
I failed to say,
"Let us do something together."
Today I said,

"I need some peace and quiet."
I failed to say,
"I am glad you are my son."
Today I said,
"Do not ever do that again."
I failed to say,
"I love you."

–Broad Street Banner

"WHAT, WHEN, IF..."

The task of protecting our children often makes us say, "Hey, don't put that in your mouth." "Be quiet." "Brush your teeth." "Don't do that." It is more effective to suggest a positive activity.

The "What, When, If" approach deals effectively with a child's behavior. The **"what"** is the task. For example, "I want you to clean your room." Or, "I want you to sweep the porch and bring in the mail." Try to be specific about what you want done, especially if the child is just learning the task. Little children may not understand something simple like, "Clean your room." We may need to say, "Pick up your toys, and put them in your toy box."

The **"when"** is a deadline. I suggest giving the child a deadline to complete the task. For instance, "I want you to take out the trash before dinner." Youngsters understand time better when it is connected to an event. For example, "I want you to play quietly until your father calls." I suggest you give teenagers a little leeway, "I want you to clean your room this weekend."

The **"if"** is a reward or consequence. For example, "If you help Mom, I will see about getting you those boots you want." Or, "If you clean your room by noon, we'll go see a movie."

"WHAT, WHEN, IF" can be a powerful tool for teaching children responsibility.

REWARDS

It is not necessary, nor wise, to reward your child every time he behaves appropriately. However, rewards are the most enduring way to influence behavior. Special treats like ordering pizza, an extra ten dollars, a new pair of shoes, or tickets to a special event encourage a child to do his best. When my daughters do well on their report cards, we plan a treat.

In our family, we give tokens, several each year, for unusual and exemplary behavior. Each token is worth about fifteen dollars. I remember giving Angi a token for being unusually nice to an injured classmate and Andi a token the first time she cooked dinner. Tokens reinforce behavior. When our daughter has five tokens, she can ask for something special. One summer the girls pooled their tokens to buy a trampoline. Another time we visited an amusement park. Look for opportunities to praise and reward your child to reinforce good behavior.

You may be thinking, "Wolfman, this is all well and good, but I'm locked up. How can I discipline my child?"

As you build a relationship with your child, by writing, calling, challenging, and rewarding, he will grow to respect your guidance. Do not let him off the hook; talk to him. The best discipline is taking time to build intimacy. Children return to affirming and intimate relationships for guidance. Remember, you are not a boss but a mentor.

EVERY FATHER NEEDS TO KNOW

Listed below are subjects that fathers need to discuss with their children. I failed the favorite subject and favorite animal questions. How could I know Andi liked monkeys?

Friends. Who is your child's best friend?
Where is your child sleeping at night?
What is his birth date? How would he like to celebrate?
What is her favorite color? Meal? Subject?
What are her dreams?
Money!
Who is his favorite band?
Does she have someone to confide in?
What does he hate? Why?
Drug abuse!
Sex and relationships! Boyfriends and girlfriends!
What does she love? Why?

Which sport does she enjoy? Which team?
If he could do anything, what would it be?
If she could live anywhere she wanted, where would it be?
Is your child happy? Why?
What makes him sad?
What makes her hurt?
What makes him afraid?
What makes her proud?
What is his favorite animal? Car? Toy?
How can you support her better?
How important is your child to you? Tell him often.
What would she like from you?
What are your dreams for your son/daughter? Tell her!
Affirm, encourage, challenge, and praise.

TOUGH LOVE

The most difficult part of discipline is dealing with unruly behavior. How do I discipline my child when he refuses to listen? This is a very difficult question asked at some point by every parent. I would encourage you to study your child's behavior and ask, "Why is he rebelling?" Try not to focus only on the behavior, whether it is lying, stealing, drug abuse, defiance, or bullying, but focus on the root cause. If your child is angry or withdrawn, he may be telling you that there is no intimacy but deep pain in the relationship. Behavioral problems are mostly the result of deep hurt, unresolved anger, bitterness, and repeated disappointment. Ask your child about his feelings, then listen. Understanding your child's feelings will help you understand the misbehavior and the resolution. Repeated behavioral problems may indicate a need to seek professional intervention and reconsider the family design. Dysfunctional children are reflections of a deeper dysfunction, and key to understanding your family.

Parents can influence the behavior of a disobedient child by offering an incentive. It is important to pick something the child will enjoy. How about playing a game, sharing a hobby, planning a special event? Learn to negotiate. For example, "If you clean your room, I'll tell your mother that she owes you—." Start small,

teach baby steps, and grant a privilege that the child will enjoy.
Slowly, negotiate for bigger goals. For instance, "The time you
spend helping your mother baby-sit, I will spend doing something special for you." Stick with age appropriate behavior, instead
of promising twelve-year-old Ricky that he can drive the car. You
must keep your promise if your child keeps his end of the bargain.
Be consistent and fair. It is especially important for parents to
spend time talking with conflicted children. Talk about your
childhood; talk about your dreams. Make time to hear his pet
peeves and anger. This will give you understanding about his
conflicts and hurt.

Discipline helps your child develop an internal code of values
while punishment imposes an external set of rules. Discipline
invites the child to reflect on his own behavior; punishment drives behavior underground. Discipline changes negative attitudes;
punishment creates resentment. Discipline offers guidelines and
limits; punishment is about pain and fear. Punishment lowers
self-esteem and destroys self-control because it is about parental
power. Discipline teaches a child to problem solve and to be
responsible.

STEPFATHERS

Dad, you may bond with a child only to discover that you are
not the natural father. Or, you may be stepfathering children from
another relationship. In either case, I encourage you not to
abruptly sever your relationship. When children invest in a relationship, they do not wait for genetic testing; children naturally
love their guardians. As a stepfather, it is important that you
support and protect the child but also defer to the natural parents.
Stepparents do not have an easy task and certainly need patience
and understanding.

CONFLICT RESOLUTION

Healthy families are not problem-free; they are problem
solvers. They communicate often and struggle to keep one
another safe. Parents must make the decision about whether to
ignore conflict, because it might go away, or confront the problem

before it becomes a crisis. Healthy families acknowledge their problems but make their home a place of warmth and encouragement.

Dysfunctional families tear themselves apart because they do not know how to end the resentment and anger. Criticism, bitterness, and blame destroy a family; nurture, care, and trust make it grow.

Every home experiences conflict. Husbands argue with wives, and children often disagree with parents. No two intelligent adults ever see eye to eye on every issue. I like Philadelphia steak hoagies; she likes chicken lo mein. However, the more often we settle our disagreements like adults, the more respect we have for one another.

CONFLICT RESOLUTION GUIDELINES:

1. Define the problem. If I go to the dentist with a toothache, and she fixes the wrong tooth, I still have a problem. Conflict cannot be resolved until both sides define the problem that they are attempting to solve.

2. List all possible solutions. Both sides must be invited to list all the possible ways the conflict might be resolved. This is an attempt to gather all the information. Invite everyone to contribute because this allows everyone to vent his or her solution. Remember that it is important to discuss the problem and not to attack each other.

3. Evaluate. Once the solutions are listed, try to find a solution everyone can agree on. Perhaps this can be achieved by combining solutions.

4. Negotiate. Negotiations toward a workable solution are not easy. It is important that both sides are allowed to save face during negotiations; otherwise, the solution will not work.

5. Commit. Use the solution, and give it time to work. If the solution fails, then reevaluate the process, and decide if you need outside intervention or if you want to start again by defining the problem.

SCREAMING

We scream when we want attention and no one is listening. Screaming is an out of control habit that leads to out of control children. Quiet consistency is far more effective. Screamers come from screaming families.

> *Do not use harmful words,*
> *But helpful words,*
> *The kind that build up and provide*
> *What is needed, so that what you say*
> *Will do good to those who hear you.*

> **–Holy Bible, Ephesians 4:29**

Discipline creates a climate of dialogue, quiet firmness, respect, and reason. This teaches a child to trust your judgment and build internal boundaries. Discipline is firm affection.

IF A CHILD LIVES WITH...

If a child lives with criticism,
  he learns to condemn.
If a child lives with hostility,
  he learns to fight.
If a child lives with fear,
  he learns to be apprehensive.
If a child lives with jealousy,
  he learns to feel guilty.
If a child lives with tolerance,
  he learns to be patient.
If a child lives with encouragement,
  he learns to be confident.
If a child lives with praise,
  he learns to be appreciative.
If a child lives with acceptance,
  he learns to love.

If a child lives with approval,
  he learns to love.
If a child lives with recognition,
  he learns it is good to have a goal.
If a child lives with honesty,
  he learns what truth is.
If a child lives with security,
  he learns to have faith in himself
  and those about him.
If a child lives with friendliness,
  he learns the world is a nice place
  in which to live.

—*Author unknown*

Chapter 10

BEAUTY

The human struggle is a quest for beauty—our own. I am referring to our inner beauty, beauty of heart and soul. The friends we select, the women we marry, and the choices we make are reflections of our life. Through dreams, creations, and desires, we call our future into being. As an example, my desire for Pam and our children led to the creation of my family. Collectively, human beings call our society and civilization into existence. We surround ourselves with the people and possessions that make us feel beautiful.

When I asked Pam to marry me, I assumed it was because I loved her. Now, I realize it was because I needed her to love me. Pam's love for me is helping me discover my inner beauty.

"Wolfman, my father told me that I would never amount to anything. I've shaken the hand of governors, but the most important day of my life was the first time my father walked through one of my factories. I wanted him to tell me that he was proud of me. He couldn't do it."

Our quest for beauty never ends. Sons, no matter their age, hunger to hear Dad say, "I am proud of you." Our desire for beauty affects our need for power, pleasure, wealth, and achievement. We find our worth and confirmation in the affirmation of those we love. In turn, creative fathers think of a thousand ways to pass on this beauty.

SYNCHRONICITY

Ande walked into my room with a letter from Ashley. His letters of confession and healing to his sixteen-year-old daughter were bringing confessions from his child. As Ande wrote to Ashley and affirmed her worth, Ashley affirmed her father. Gradually, both father and daughter began to glow, reflecting the beauty they shared. I could see Ashley's beauty in Ande's smile.

I was drawn into the process. As Ande and I talked, I reflected on the synchronicity (mysterious coincidence of events) of my own life. I now know there is a transparent thread that runs through life. My healing affects my daughters and wife, just as their healing affects me. James Hillman says, "We can go with another only as far as we have gone with ourselves."

Synchronicity is beyond anything we could ever imagine. We create our destiny, and then our destiny creates us. We dare to dream, and before long we are caught in the universal drama.

RIVERS AND ROCKS

The river cuts her way through the rock, sometimes meandering along, other times rushing passionately toward the sea. In time, the river changes everything; nothing can remain in her path. Rivers are passionate and changing.

Rocks shoulder the river. Like eternal watchmen, they guard the river even as she grinds them away in merciless passion. Without rock our land would be flat, covered with a great ocean. Rocks offer the river a channel of stability and hope.

Rocks and rivers need each other, even though the battle never ends. The river pounds the rock, but they belong together; identity comes from the struggle.

Rivers have a motto, "You live only once."
Rocks have a motto, "Better safe than sorry."

Rivers and rocks remind me of people. Some people are passionate, impulsive and changing. Others are firm, unmovable, and enduring. River people complain to rock people, "If you weren't so predictable, we could have some fun." Or, "I'm bored with the same old, same old." Not to be out done, rock people remind river people, "You upset my schedule." Or, "If we did it your way, we would be up the creek." And the argument continues....

...Until one day when the river and rock realize that they need each other. No matter how much we grind against each other and bitterly complain, river people bring life, and rock people hold it together. The unity of river and rock brings growth and wholeness. We compliment and complete one another even as we strive for fulfillment. Unity creates balance. And in this moment of awareness, the river and the rock find harmony.

Harmony? How could anyone know the river and rock have made peace? Music! Walk on the rock, along the river, and listen to the harmony of rock and river together. It is a symphony.

Fathers need children, children need fathers, husbands need wives, and wives need husbands. The circle of life is a struggle, and it is never complete, but there is harmony.

RIVERS

Changing	Impulsive	Transparent	Jubilant
Passionate	Fluid	Alive	
Flowing	Exciting	Carefree	

ROCKS

Predictable	Solid	Firm	Opaque
Stable	Enduring	Dependable	

DOTTIE

Dottie was an imperfect lady; like most of us, she struggled with the balance of river and rock. Cancer stole her breasts and chemo, her hair. We were attending a friend's wedding reception when Dottie decided to be a "river" and dance. Her neck puffed with cancer, she dragged her young but worn body onto the dance floor for one last defiant stand against the oppressing disease. We watched her spin and twirl, mostly on raw courage. And then, as she danced, Dottie's brown wig shifted and spun until it covered her eyes. She never missed a beat. As the wig turned and exposed her thinning hair, Dottie danced. I was embarrassed and tried to hide it with laughter. I remembered Dottie walking the subways of Philadelphia to give homeless people coffee, sandwiches, hot spaghetti, and blankets. I remembered her quick laugh and beautiful smile, now twisted by her swollen neck and exhaustion. I saw the emptiness of missing breasts and sinking eyes. I remembered and laughed as Dottie danced...and danced...and laughed...and laughed...and then we cried.

When I first met her, she was robust, energetic, passionate, and beautiful. Her husband and children called her blessed. In the battle with cancer, Dottie lost the outward features of beauty. Her face paled as her eyes darkened. But the smile of the woman I had first known was innocent and superficial when compared to the smile of the suffering woman. In the fight for life, Dottie grasped understanding. Her outward beauty and naïveté were replaced by the truth of suffering. She lost the fight with cancer, but she won the battle for beauty.

People are like stained glass windows: They sparkle and shine when the sun is out, but when the darkness sets in, their true beauty is revealed only if there is a light from within.

–Elizabeth Kubler-Ross

ENOUGH ALREADY

The battle between us is petty when compared to the struggle that unites us. When will we learn to stop bullying each other and learn to make beauty like the rock and river? East against west, north against south, black against white, men against men, men against women, prisoner against guard, human against human. Enough already!–and for what purpose? Is this really the world of conflict that we want to create for our children?

You have been chosen by God who has given you this new kind of life, and because of God's deep love and concern for you, you should practice tenderhearted mercy and kindness to others

–Holy Bible, Colossians 3:12

HEADED TOWARD LOVE

Beauty begins with love. Beauty never occurs in isolation because love is interactive. How will we find our beauty in prison? When the love bottled inside reaches out to ease the struggle and pain of others, we find beauty and life. Bank accounts and power are cheap imitations. Tear off the blinders and look around; reach beyond the narrow confines of the self to lift others. Beauty is not victory for the self but victory of the Self.

My ancestors dreamed of a destiny that has been passed to me. Someday, when I sit by the eternal fire of my family, the elders will look at me and smile. I want the smile to be one of pride and not pity, of joy and not sorrow, of hope and not despair. My ancestors led me to prison so I could learn about fatherhood, respect, and beauty.

Men of beauty have been forged on the dark steel of prison. I have met a few of these men: Peru, Seer, Tony, Kevin, Cesar, Tyrone, Murph, Delbert, Michael, Jack, and John...they have changed my life. When I first began teaching, I assumed that I would be instructing hard prisoners about family life. Instead, inmates have taught me about suffering and hope, loss and freedom, humiliation and dignity. I have watched prisoners carry each other's burden and hurt. When we learn to carry each other's burden and feel each other's pain, injustice will flee and a new day of beauty will dawn.

Henry James, when asked by his nephew about what he ought to do with his life, said, "Three things are important. The first is to be kind. The second is to be kind. And the third is to be kind."

RISING UP...

On the day of beauty, we will wipe out indifference, hunger, and abuse. Fear and violence will flee before the dawn of justice and understanding. Indifference brings war and prison, hate and injustice, crime and abuse. On the day of beauty, we will not be judged by the color of our skin, our gender, education, or wealth. We will destroy all the reasons for war and embrace the inevitable —LOVE. When we have suffered enough, love will determine what is just and unjust. Love creates beauty.

I am going to ask you to join me in the following pledge:

F-A-T-H-E-R-S UNITE: I will be Faithful and Affectionate to my child. I will Talk with him/her and develop a Healing relationship. I will be Empathetic, Respectful and Supportive. Namaste!

In the process of commitment to your family, you may discover that men of character and beauty are even now being hammered on the forge of dark prison steel. You are the generation that can offer new life to two million children, children damned to repeat the cycle unless you accept the challenge.

Ryan said, "If you don't write the book, Mr. Wolfman, someone else will." Gentlemen, if you neglect your responsibility, someone else will play your drama. Do not lose your opportunity to care because you wallow in self-pity. I encourage you, accept responsibility for your life and children. Be a friend, be a mentor. Gather all the love of your ancestors inside of you and share it. Become the kind of father and friend you need: accepting, affectionate, and beautiful.

ROCKS AND RIVERS

Rivers ramble relentlessly forward
Sometimes stormy and seething,
Often trickling and tired, serene
From warm water waving wet fingers,
Sharp rocks soon become smooth and silky.

–Andi Wolfgang

POSTLUDE

I walked into my Parenting III class one afternoon concerned about my daughter. She was nearing the end of her first year in college and facing decisions that would affect her future. During the ten-minute break, Foster asked, "What's on your mind, Mr. Wolfgang? You don't seem to be here today."

I mumbled, "It is one thing to teach Parenting and another to worry about my own children."

I will never forget Foster's response, "Mr. Wolfgang, let me teach you something that you taught me...and forgot."

Mr. Foster hit the nail on the head. I had forgotten! The lessons that I was teaching fell away when I was faced with concerns in my own family. Foster went on to say that the gift of respect, intimacy, and beauty always triumph. However, in moments of panic we forget and return to the traps of fear, blame, anger, and control.

Here I was teaching men in our Parenting III class about fatherhood, and I had lost my footing. Foster, doing nearly eighteen years of time, refreshed my memory.

Over the last ten chapters, we have traveled together across awareness, self, consciousness, lifestyle, intimacy, spirituality, respect, discipline, communication, and beauty. I have been privileged to be a guide. Now I know that I will forget parts of the journey. But my children, grandchildren, and great grandchildren need guidance. Your children and grandchildren must also learn the way. Become a guide; teach me what I have forgotten.

Write to me. Tell me about your journey, your family, and your hope. Show me the path. If I write again, may I consider your contributions for publication?

Thanks for inviting me to share your valuable time. I pray that your beauty will be reflected back to you. Namaste!

Love and peace,
Wolfman

Wolfman • Stone Creek • RR 2, Box 110 • Paxinos, PA 17860